A HISTORY OF PARBOLD

A History of Parbold

J. M. VIRGOE

Carnegie Publishing, 1994

A History of Parbold
by J. M. Virgoe

Published by Carnegie Publishing, 1994

Typeset in Monotype Bembo by Carnegie Publishing Ltd
18 Maynard St, Preston, Lancs.
Printed and bound in the UK by T. Snape & Co., Preston

British Library Cataloguing in Publication Data
A CIP record for this book is available from the British Library

ISBN 0-948789-77-8

Contents

Acknowledgements

THE raw material on which this book is based has been collected over several years. The main debt is owed to the staff of the Lancashire Record Office, Preston, without whose help none of it would have been possible. Important contributions have been made by the staffs of the Wigan Record Office, Leigh, and the Lancashire County Library both in Ormskirk and Skelmersdale. Several other people have contributed to a lesser extent in numerous small ways. To all my thanks.

When the book was in the later stages of preparation a local history group was set up in Parbold under the leadership of Dr Mary Bonsall. This group has concentrated on the mid-nineteenth century. As far as possible I have attempted not to use to any great extent information from this group, whose work will, hopefully, be published elsewhere. Nonetheless I would like to acknowledge the added stimulus I have received from my membership of this group.

This book can only be considered to be a beginning into the study of the local history of Parbold. Many readers will doubtless have additional information and will recognise omissions and errors in the contents. I will be grateful for any corrections or further information.

J. M. Virgoe
Parbold, September 1989

Burscough Priory.
All that remains of the priory associated with the earliest history of Parbold are these two columns.

Preface

PARBOLD is first mentioned in the documents of Burscough Priory and Cockersand Abbey at the turn of the twelfth and thirteenth centuries. It subsequently became one of the four townships in the parish of Eccleston along with Heskin, Wrightington and Eccleston itself. Many Lancashire parishes did not conform to the pattern of the 'typical' English parish-village with a village centred around the parish church, village green and pond, and with a manor broadly equating to the same area, and with clearly defined boundaries separating it from the next parish-village. Lancashire parishes were frequently much bigger and comprised more than one village centre or township.

The management of local affairs was divided between the mother parish, exercising control through the vestry, and the township through its locally appointed officers such as the constable and the surveyor of the highways. The township in Lancashire thus carried out many, but not all, of the functions exercised by the parish in other parts of the country. Parbold was such a township, and remained so until the Local Government Act of 1894, when it became a civil parish in its own right. These two dates, defining a period of nearly seven hundred years, form the framework within which the major part of this story is confined. Throughout this period the population of the township never exceeded 600.

Most of Parbold was owned by the Lathom family of Parbold up to the Civil War, after which it was confiscated. Although the Lathoms recovered it for a short while afterwards, it was subsequently purchased by John Crisp, whose descendants sold it to William Dicconson (1727–1801) of Wrightington. William Dicconson died without children and Parbold passed to his brother Edward, who in turn died childless. The estate then passed to his nephew Thomas Eccleston and thence to his younger son Charles (1801–60), who on inheriting Wrightington and Parbold took the name Dicconson.

He subsequently inherited Scarisbrick in 1833. As Charles Scarisbrick he had considerable wealth, and was considered to be one of the richest commoners in Lancashire. This convoluted family history is useful because the majority of the original documents relating to the history of Parbold are to be found either in the Dicconson Papers (DDWr) at the Wigan Record Office, Leigh or in the Scarisbrick papers (DDSc) at the Lancashire Record Office, Preston. A minor, but important landowner in the village was Hesketh of Rufford, and additional sources are to be found in the Hesketh Papers (DDHe) at Preston.

The story is essentially a local one: national events, particularly the Civil Wars and the siege of nearby Lathom House clearly affected the township, but their contribution to the recorded history is relatively small. Similarly, the main road from Scotland to the south, trod by the Jacobites in 1715 and again in 1745, passes only a few miles away at Standish, but there is little record of what impact, if any, these events had upon the inhabitants of Parbold.

One curious reminder of national events remains at 'Parbold Bottle'. This monument was erected to commemorate the 1832 Parliamentary Reform Act, but why and by whom it was erected does not appear to be recorded.

Charles Scarisbrick, 1801–1860

Parbold 'Bottle'. Built to commemorate the Reform Act 1832, and restored in 1958. The view shows the flat West Lancashire Plain with Parbold Village at the break of slope.

I

The Village

THE NATURAL LANDSCAPE

PARBOLD is situated on the extreme edge of the south-west Lancashire plain. Part is on the plain itself and part is on the hills rising from it, including Parbold Hill which rises to nearly four hundred feet. Parbold village straddles the fifty-foot contour, whilst to the south and west the Douglas Valley occupies the lowest lying land liable to winter flooding.

The village lies on the western edge of the south Lancashire coalfield and is underlain by rocks of the Lower Coal Measures, consisting of shales and sandstones, with occasional thin coal seams which in the eighteenth and nineteenth centuries supported three small collieries in the village. The sandstones, particularly a coarse, gritty rock known as the Harrock Hill Grit, are generally more resistant to erosion and form the backbone of the ridge of higher land running from Harrock Hill through Hunter's Hill, Hawett Hill and Parbold Hill. The Harrock Hill Grit provided the basis of the quarrying industry of the area.

The Coal Measures are mostly overlain by boulder clay, which was laid down as a superficial deposit by the ice sheets of the last Ice Age. This is absent in some areas—mainly on the higher land—where the soil is developed directly on the Coal Measure rocks. The boulder clay is generally very impermeable and gives rise to heavy, poorly drained soils. The boulder clay has also modified the terrain by smoothing out the irregularities of the pre-existing landscape. Parbold Hill would almost certainly appear steeper were it not for the boulder clay which is deposited against it. The higher land is found in the north east of the district. Parbold Hill is a well-known vantage point giving extensive views over the south-west Lancashire plain and to the hills of North Wales.

It seems probable that before the activities of man all of the area was covered by woodland. Numerous trees still give an impression of the district being well-wooded on the slopes east of Parbold village, whilst Wood Lane, although previously known as Rough Hey Lane, marks the location of a fairly extensive wood which was in existence in the late eighteenth century. At what stage the clearance of the bulk of the woodland took place is not clear. Early documents [1,2] refer to Award's Assart,* Esward's Assart and Warin's Assart in the thirteenth century. Similarly, the use of 'hurst' in place names such as Lighthurst and Fernyhurst implies the existence of woodland in former times.

BEGINNINGS

There is little or no evidence of human occupation in the Parbold area before the Conquest, although there undoubtedly would have been a small number of people living in the district at that time. The only possible indication of prehistoric man is the mound known as Boar's Den, a knoll some thirty yards across and rising fifteen feet above the surrounding land. Boar's Den is described vaguely as a tumulus on the Ordnance Survey map, but it has never been properly investigated.

Although the Roman road from Warrington to Lancaster passes only five miles to the east, there is no direct evidence of a Roman presence in Parbold. That they left the road and went into the hinterland from time to time is shown, however, by the finding of a hoard of 110 Roman coins at nearby Lathom in 1949. But there was little reason for them to visit the region: the surrounding area was in part heavily wooded, and elsewhere bleak moorland and without known mineral wealth. The population was sparse. However, it should be noted that the lack of documentary and archaeological evidence for pre-conquest settlement—a county-wide problem—does not necessarily mean that such settlement was absent. Rather, it indicates how much research and investigation remains to be done in Lancashire. Even by the time of the Domesday survey in 1086, settlement appears of have been mainly confined to the

---

* An assart was a clearance within generally wooded land.

coastal areas of West Derby Hundred, there being very little habitation in what would later become known as South Lancashire, west of a line through Tarbock and passing through Skelmersdale. Although the Domesday Book is far from complete, it seems certain that there were no main centres of population, which probably only numbered a thousand or two living in scattered rural communities. There is no mention of Parbold at all in the Domesday survey, although it has been suggested that 'Bold' or 'Botl' names are from Old English meaning *a dwelling*, and could point to a seventh- or eighth-century origin.[3] Parbold is first recorded in 1195 as Iperbolt, changing through Perebold (1202), Perbold (1212), Perbalt and Perbald (1292).[4] The name has been said to mean 'the place where pears grow'.[5]

The place-names of south Lancashire show evidence of sixth- and seventh-century English settlement largely to the east of the Parbold area, the unreclaimed moss lands to the west showing little evidence of habitation. By the ninth and tenth centuries, the Scandinavian settlers had come into the region; place-name evidence suggesting that their influence was largely restricted to the hitherto uninhabited western areas.[6] Parbold is located at about the line where these two cultures met.

The nearest places to Parbold recorded in the Domesday Book are Lathom, largely wooded, Dalton, Skelmersdale and Upholland.[7] All except Upholland were in the possession of Ughtred, who held seventeen manors in the West Derby Hundred. Although the descent is speculative, it has been suggested that the Lathom family, who were to become the principal landowners in the area, were the direct descendants of Ughtred, who was almost certainly a Saxon lord.

Following the Conquest, William had given the bulk of the area between the Ribble and the Mersey to one of his supporters, Roger of Poitou, who built his castle at Penwortham. Parbold and Wrightington, whose histories as we shall see are closely interlinked, were within the Barony of Manchester, which was held in turn by the Grelley family. From Albert Grelley, who died about 1162, Wrightington is said to have passed to Orm, the possible founder of Ormskirk. By the mid-thirteenth century Parbold was held by the Lathom family of Parbold, who held it of the Barony of Manchester

Boar's Den, showing the elevation of this apparent tumulus mound above the surrounding level.

in return for the services of one-fourth part of a knight, the other three-fourths being given in return for Wrightington and which possibly included Dalton.

THE EARLY VILLAGE

The first references to Parbold appear in the documents of nearby Burscough Priory, and the more distant Cockersand Abbey, located on a remote and windswept part of the Lancashire coast south of Lancaster. Grants of land in Parbold were made to the two religious houses at the turn of the twelfth and thirteenth centuries. The earliest reference actually appears to be in 1180, when Henry of Parbold witnessed a gift of four acres of land in Ulnes Walton to the monks of Cockersand. Bulpit [8] claims that William Gillibrand, who witnessed a deed in 1190 to a grant of land in Eccleston, was from Parbold, but whilst it would be nice to be able to link this individual with the present Gillibrand's Farm in Parbold, the evidence that he was from Parbold seems to be lacking, and he is perhaps more likely to be connected to the Gillibrands of Chorley.

Henry of Parbold is mentioned in several of these early documents

Cockersand Abbey. The ruins of this remote religious house situated south west of Lancaster. The main feature is the Chapter House.

covering a period up to about 1240. The documents are too numerous to quote in full, but the example gives a good indication of the information they contain.

> Grant from Henry de Parbold to God and St Mary of Cockersand of a certain portion of his land in Parbold within these bounds. From the Risen Bridge down the Main Gate to the land of St John, follow that land to the syke which is the boundary of the land of Robert de Linleys, and so going up that syke to Risen Bridge again; with common of pasture and other easements of the town of Parbold belonging to so much land, and acquaintance of pannage for the demesne pigs of the men dwelling upon that land.

This document is interesting in that it refers to a bridge in the village, several pointers as to places, and also to the land of Robert de Linleys, which can be connected to the area of the present-day Lindley Hotel. The land of St John is a reference to land owned in the area by the Knights of St John of Jerusalem. This was a monastic order founded at the end of the eleventh century whose members wore a black habit with an eight-pointed star on the breast. The order rapidly spread all over Europe and acquired considerable lands by gift.

Extracts from other deeds of this period give a good description of numerous boundaries:

> West side of Fernley Clough between Award's Assart and Douglas Water.

> Green Leach into Lichthurst Clough, up Lichthurst Clough eastwards to the cross, then follow the ditch to another cross in Haverhole Carr into the Green Leach again.

> One acre in Parbold above the Ferneyhurst Lamilade and Little Lichthurst.

> Beginning at the watercourse towards the south, follow the water course to a ditch towards the west, and by that ditch towards the north . . . and also another land where Lintlehecloh [Lindley Clough] falls into the Douglas, follow the Douglas round to Scatdepul, follow Scatdepul to Lantpul, follow Lantpul down to Lintlehecloh to the Douglas.

> An assart in Parbold between Esward's Assart and Deadmansyke; from the Carr at the lower end, round Deadmansyke to Annianastub

> at the higher end. An other assart next to the road from Walton Lees as Roger's Boundary goes in the higher head to Halliwelle Cliffe to the lower side of Warin's Assart, across to Letha Gat, by Letha Gat to Rot Fallan Hac . . .

No attempt has been made to identify in detail the places mentioned, but Ferneyhurst has been equated with Fairhurst,[9] an ancient cross which stood until the end of the last century at the bottom of Stoney Lane. 'Leach' is a stream flowing through boggy ground, and 'pul' is the confluence of a stream with a river. The general impression is that the area in question is on the north side of the present village.

FIELD NAMES

The Hesketh of Rufford held land in Parbold, and within the documents of the Hesketh deposited at the Lancashire Record Office, a number of deeds give field names which can be traced over several centuries.

Kay's Crook, for example, is listed as lot seven in the particulars of land offered for sale in 1875.[10] It is also shown on the accompanying map, which enables it to be located as behind the area

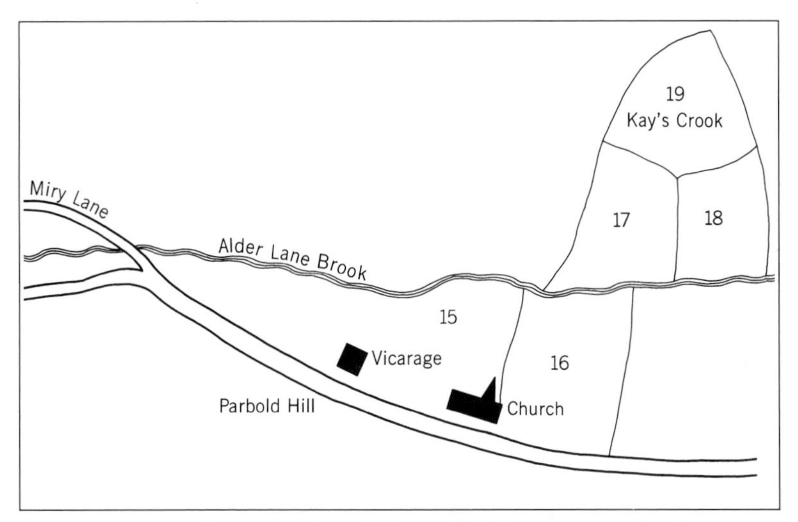

Location of Kay's Crook. A field traceable back to 1391. Map based on details of land for sale 1875 (LRO DDHe 96/9).

which subsequently was to become the site of Christ Church, Parbold. In a survey of 1818 [11] there is an area referred to as Carse Crook, which may or may not refer to the same plot, but a document [12] of 1569 provides the key, when it refers to 'Kayes Croke alias Carescroke and Dobbe Heys being part of a messuage called Hasylcarre House'. In 1488 [13] we find Carles Crokes and Doblehey, and as far back as 1391,[14] 'a place of land and waste called Cayescroke in Perbalt'. Thus we are able to trace this particular field over nearly six hundred years, and, moreover, to locate it accurately. 'Dob' or 'Dobbe' is said to be an old form of Robert,[15] and could possibly refer to the Robert de Linley mentioned earlier.

The same sale documents of 1875 also enable fields to be located close to the present-day *Rigby Arms*, which can be traced back, with similar changes in spelling, to documents of 1593; Milners Acre of 1593 becoming Millers Acre, Watbanke changing to Wandbank and Kockeshites becoming Cockshoot. Ekwall,[9] in his book on the place-names of Lancashire, claims that the word cockshoot occurs in documents back to the late twelfth century, and means a glade through which woodcocks or other birds might dart and could be caught by stretching nets across the opening. This also implies that the area on the side of Parbold Hill referred to in the document was at some time prior to 1593 partly wooded.

MAPS

The geography of the landscape as it was in former times can in part be deduced from the physical remains existing today, but also from the information available from contemporary maps. Although Parbold, or at least Douglas Chapel, is shown on most of the early county maps, these are by no means accurate surveys but, at best, pictorial representations of the landscape. The first really useful map is that of Yates, published in 1786. This shows the road pattern in the area much as it is today, with about twenty-two identifiable houses shown in the Parbold area. Yates also shows two watermills, Douglas Mill on the river just north of Parbold Bridge, and a watermill just below Fairhurst Hall. Strictly speaking, the latter is in Wrightington, but it is right on the township boundary.

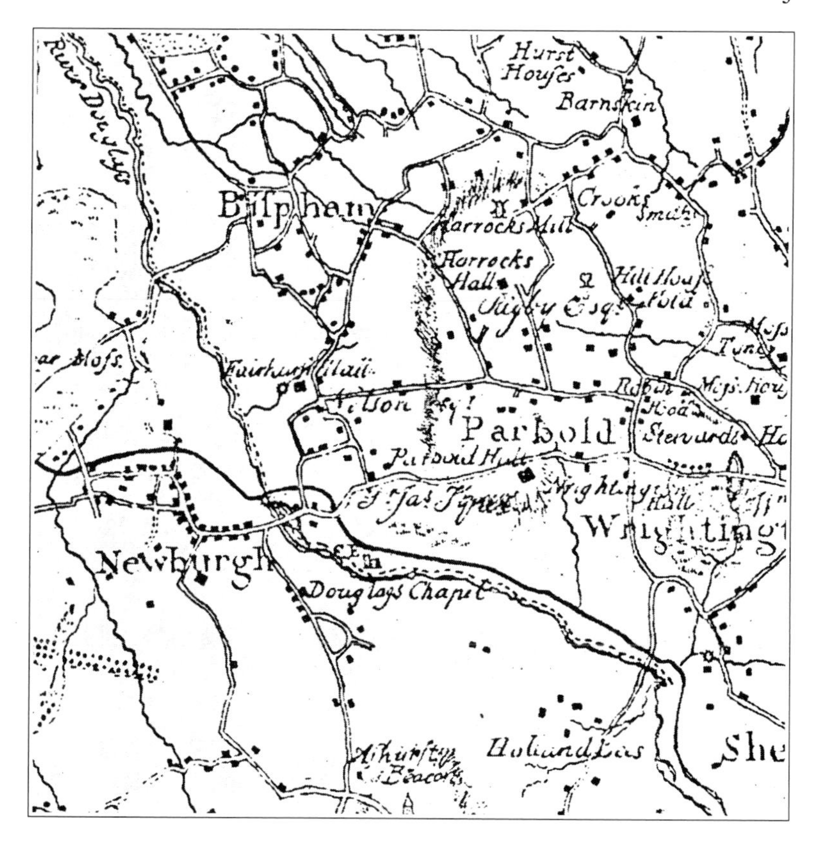

Part of Yates' map of Lancashire (1786), showing the Parbold area.

Produced in the same year as Yates' map is a larger-scale and much more detailed map showing the estates of the Misses Tyrell.[16] This is an excellent map and covers most of Parbold, but, being an estate map, there are gaps on it where the land did not belong to the Misses Tyrell. A further estate map, this time showing the small Gillibrand estate, is also helpful for that area.[17] This is undated, but is probably from about 1809.

The first large-scale and detailed map of the township is that of the tithe survey made in 1837. This map, together with the accompanying schedule,[18] shows and names every field, house, boundary and building, together with the names of the owner and occupier and, in most cases, the use to which the land was put. It was followed shortly after by the first 6-inch map of the Ordnance

Survey in 1846, and then by the 25-inch map in 1894. We can, therefore, get a detailed idea of what the village looked like over the last two hundred years.

PARBOLD BRIDGE

The thirteenth-century charters of Cockersand Abbey refer several times to a bridge, the Risen Bridge, in Parbold. The exact location of this bridge is not known, but in all probability it would have been located close to the existing bridge on the road to Newburgh. The Douglas would have provided a barrier to movement in this direction, but the connection with Burscough Priory, the attraction of a weekly market at Newburgh, as well as the more glamorous attraction of a chartered market town at Ormskirk, would all have demanded some means of crossing the river. There is no evidence for suggesting an alternative location to the present one, and further evidence is forthcoming from the late nineteenth century: when Parbold Bridge was rebuilt with iron girders, it was found that the old stone bridge was supported on older, wooden piles.[19]

Douglas Bridge is mentioned in a will of 1369 when Thomas de Lathom left eleven marks 'ad Pont de Doggles', and again in 1401, when Alexander Pyk gave two acres of land in Dalton by 'Doggles Bridge' for life and after his death, towards the repair of the 'bridge of Doggles' for ever.

Repairing the bridge was a regular item; money was again spent in 1658 [20] and in 1707,[21] the latter repair being estimated at £150. Both these repairs are clearly identified with the present bridge site, since the bridge is described as 'Douglas Bridge between Lathom and Parbold'. The bridge was again in a poor state of repair in 1752, when an order [22] was made at the quarter sessions for the battlements on the bridge to be raised at the joint expense of the inhabitants of the hundreds of West Derby and Leyland, because the public 'are in danger of their lives in crossing'. The river was the ancient boundary between these two hundreds.

Newburgh was at that time part of the township of Lathom within the parish of Ormskirk. Although Parbold and Newburgh were in two distinct townships in two different parishes and hundreds, and with different ancestral lords of the manor, there is evidence that from time to time the distinction was blurred. For example, the cornmill in the centre of Parbold was shown on the Ordnance Survey map as Newburgh Mill; the adjacent canal bridge was shown on the 1837 tithe map as Newburgh Bridge; the station in Parbold was on occasion described as Newburgh station, and the quarries on Hunter's Hill as being near Newburgh.

THE ROADS

The condition of the roads was always a concern in the days before tarmacadam roads were developed, and the only labour available to repair them was the muscle of the local people. Even though the amount of traffic was negligible, winter rains, poor drainage and the narrow wheels of horse or oxen-drawn carts served to turn them into pot-holed, rutted, muddy tracks. The surveyor of the highways was an important local officer burdened with the task of extracting labour from a frequently far from willing local workforce.

The earliest known mention of the roads in Parbold is in 1634,[23] when it was agreed at a general meeting of the inhabitants of Wrightington and Parbold that a tax should be raised for the repair of the road between the two townships (now the A5209).

We know that problems continued by a further reference in 1780,[24] when James Bradshaw was surveyor for the highways. The roads were in poor condition and six pence in the pound was to be raised from the inhabitants, occupants and owners of land, houses, tenements and heriditaments or any personal estate, to be used for 'amending, repairing, paving, clearing and supporting the said highways'. Bradshaw was to collect the money and, if not paid within ten days, was to sell the goods of defaulters. Any improvement there may have been was short-lived; at the quarter sessions held on 15 May 1794,[25] the inhabitants of Parbold were indicted for not repairing the road from the Leeds and Liverpool Canal bridge and running towards Ormskirk for a length of 220 yards by eight yards wide. The indictment apparently had an effect, for at the sessions on 9 October the road was reported to have been 'well and sufficiently repaired'.

Yet again, in October 1800,[26] the inhabitants were presented for non-repair of the highway from a bridge or culvert recently made at the end of the township towards Newburgh for a length of highway one hundred yards long by ten feet wide. A fine was threatened at the next session, but a request was made and granted for further time as the repair was going on as fast as it could.

In 1813 a warrant of apprehension 'of two substantial men', Thomas Liptrot and Thomas Barton, was issued for non-repair of the highway.[27] The road in question extended from two roods below the school on Parbold Hill, ending at the brook which divides Parbold and Wrightington, a total length of 38 roods (about 210 yards). The reference here is not to the school on Parbold Hill, which was not built until the 1870s, but probably to Parbold Hall, which was a school early in the nineteenth century.

The roads were also a matter of local dispute in 1682, when John Crisp of Parbold Hall was presented at the quarter sessions for setting up an obstruction in a lane called Parbold Lane, whereby the inhabitants were unable to pass freely by with carts and carriages. John Crisp was ordered to remove the obstruction under the penalty of a hefty fine, and a certificate of compliance was issued at Ormskirk Sessions in 1683.[28]

Some local roads were not repaired by the public at large, because they were a private responsibility. Thus, the lane leading down to Douglas Chapel was looked after by the chuchwardens with the help of the pottery nearby, as an entry in the back of the baptism register of the chapel reads:[29]

> At a meeting in the vestry at this chapel holden this day by public notice for that purpose, it was agreed that the road from the Chapel Lane gate down to the canal bridge shall be repaired by the wardens for the parish and be authorised to charge the same to the parish account, excepting so much thereof as shall be judged equitable to be paid towards the expense thereof by the occupant of the pottery there.

The entry was signed by Rigbye Rigbye, Edward Dicconson and John Anderton.

16- AND 17-CENTURY PARBOLD

A surviving list of rentals of the land in Lancashire owned by the Order of St John, dating from about the year 1540,[30] gives considerable information concerning the land holdings, holders and values for Wrightington and Parbold. The family names include many which recur throughout the centuries, while many of the places mentioned are also found in other documents and some can be identified today. The full list was:

Nicholas Rigby for 1 messuage called Haroc	5*s*. 6*d*.
Ralph Standish for Han Hey in Wrightington	1*d*.(?)
James Barton for Lyndly Close	8*s*.
Katherine relict of William Howet for a messuage called Le Croke	12*d*.
Richard Banastre for a messuage in Parbold called Bewhous	11*d*.
Nicholas Richardson for one messuage	12*d*.
Thomas Westhed for one messuage	12*d*.
Robert Smith for 1 messuage	4*d*.
Margery relict of John Strange for one messuage	20*d*.
Richard Latham Esq. for . . . pul in the tenure of the chaplain of Dugles	6*d*.
Edward, Earl of Derby for 1 messuage	2*d*.
Bartholmew Hesket for Barker feld	4*d*.
Thomas Stopford for Dobhey	11*d*.
Richard Banester for 1 messuage	4*d*.
Richard Latham Esq. for brodfeld	6*d*.
For part of Fisherfeld	2*d*.
Nicholas Haliwel for a messuage called Dunser Hous	6*d*.
James Scarsbrec for 2 crofts called Cristians and Pighye	11*d*.
The heirs of Thomas Banester of Lostoc for lands and tenements	16*d*.

A detailed account of Parbold as it was in 1623 is given in the *inquisition post mortem* of Thomas Lathum taken at Wigan on 25 September in that year.[31] His estate comprised a large house, twelve smaller houses, eight cottages, a watermill and some 407 acres. All the houses and cottages had gardens and orchards, and the land was described variously as 'land' (130 acres), 'meadow' (35 acres), 'pasture' (215 acres), 'wood' (50 acres), and 'heath and briar' (40 acres). Forty acres of this property formerly belonged to the Chantry of 'Dugles'. Although much of the land had been cleared by this time, twenty-two per cent of the area was still given over to woodland or 'heath and briar', and it is clear that the work of improving the land still had some way to go. Nevertheless, the description creates a picture of a pastoral landscape of dwellings with small gardens and orchards which produced food for the inhabitants. However, the acreage accounted for in this description is less than half the total area of the township.

A similar inquisition relating to Robert Hesketh of Rufforth (Rufford), coincidentally also taken in 1623,[32] accounts for a further 54 acres, and adds to our knowledge another three houses in the village, but there is still a considerable acreage unaccounted for. In all probability the small Gillibrand estate of some 28 acres or so was separate, as we shall see later.

REMAINS OF THE OLD VILLAGE

With the demolition of Douglas Chapel in 1878, the stone from which was used to build the new school on Parbold Hill, there are now no visible physical remains of Parbold dating from earlier than the late seventeenth century. The surviving stone houses are of that period, two with date stones being Common House (1692), and Manor Cottage (1686). Gillibrand House, which is in all probability an ancient site, has a brick façade of apparently Georgian appearance, although the rear of the house is in stone. Recent restoration work has revealed an earlier, inner house within the existing structure.

The tithe map of 1837 [33] shows the hamlet close to Gillibrands as containing seven cottages, which in 1851 were occupied by a total of forty persons.[34] By 1871[35] the population had dropped to 31, the majority of the men working in the quarries. Today, only traces of walling within the bracken and trees show where this small community once stood. Similarly, the hamlet at New Cotts Fold, which is situated a few hundred yards north of Parbold Hall, has reverted to a wild state, and must be unrecognised as a former site of human occupation by almost all who pass along the narrow footpath going through it.

Chapel House, too, was formerly an area of greater importance, with Douglas Chapel; a pottery situated close by in the early nineteenth century; and *Chapel House Inn*, run latterly by the Southport Brewery Company. All these buildings have long since disappeared. The previous importance of Douglas Chapel, and the way in which it served the countryside round about, can be gauged by the way that footpaths converge upon the site from Newburgh, Dalton and the Appley Bridge direction, including the crossing of the river by a footbridge (though the present one is a modern replacement).

There is no trace today of the Parbold Hall of the Lathoms, and Price [36] considers its location to be uncertain. However, there would seem to be little reason for believing it to be anywhere other than on or near to the site of the present hall. The current hall was probably built about 1730–50 for Thomas Crisp, successor to John Crisp and Member of Parliament for Ilchester in Somerset, whose crest, a camelopard, is carved upon the pediment.[37] This building was probably a reconstruction of an earlier one; the current north front certainly shows two window levels which appear to represent two phases of building.

Other historic buildings, all traces of which have disappeared in the last hundred years or so, include the water corn mill which stood on the Douglas just north of the bridge on the Parbold–Newburgh boundary. A second watermill, of which, again, all traces

Gillibrand House prior to recent restoration, showing a stone gable end and brick 'Georgian' frontage.

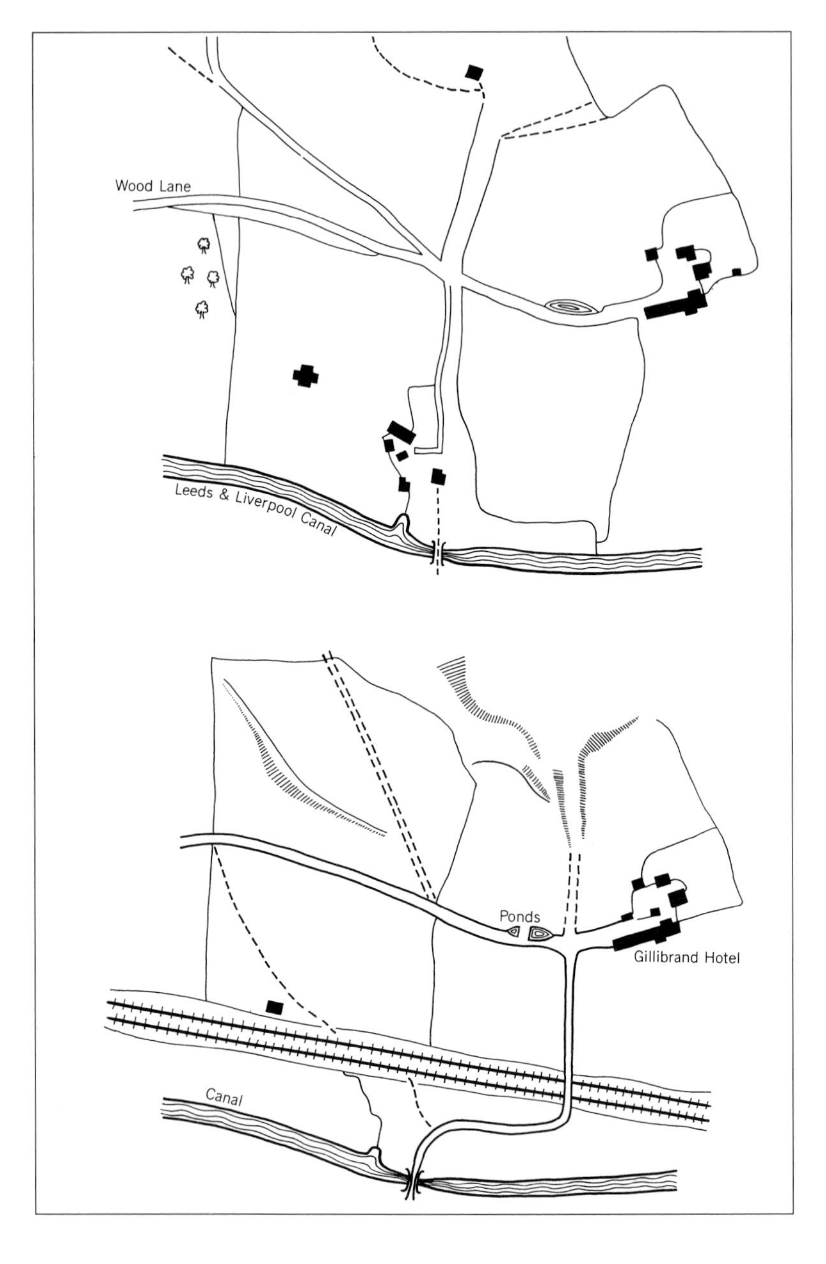

Changes in the Gillibrands area 1837–1894. A comparison of the tithe map of 1837 and the Ordnance Survey map of 1894 shows the disappearance of the hamlet, the building of the railway, the development of spoil banks from quarrying, and a rearrangement of the lanes.

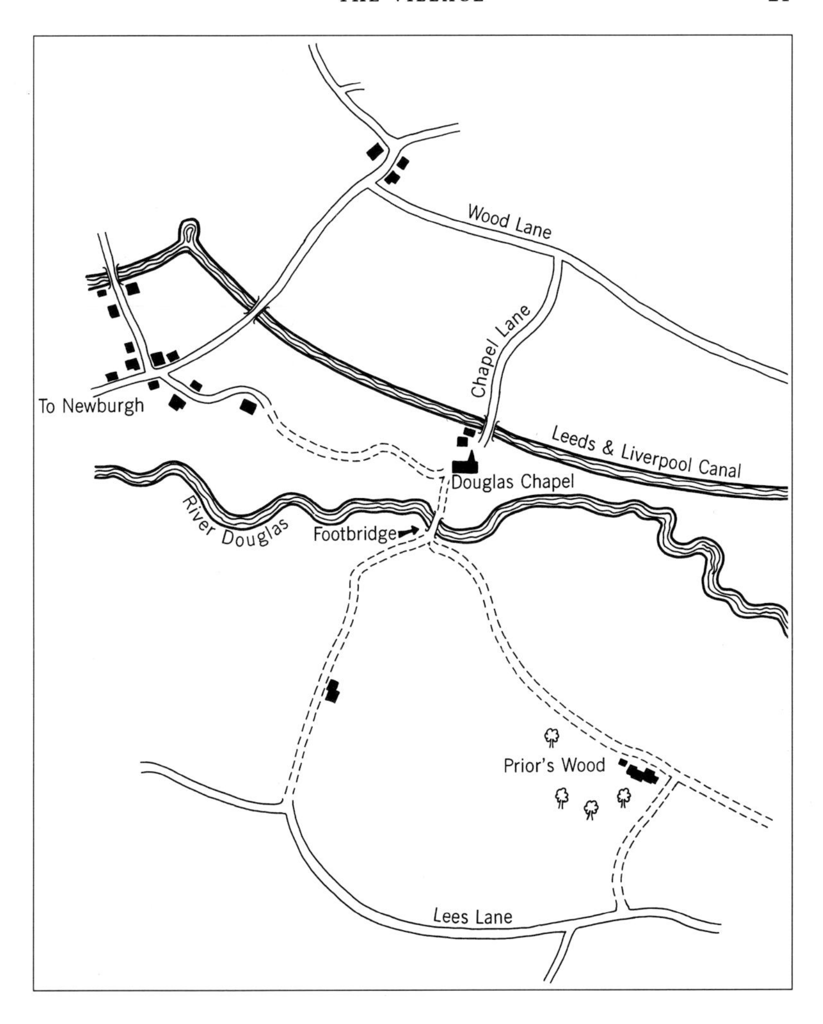

Map showing the convergence of routes on Douglas Chapel. (Based on OS map 1846)

have long since gone, was located on a stream just below Fairhurst Hall and close to the township boundary.

THE NAVIGATIONS

At the beginning of the eighteenth century the state of the roads was so poor as to constitute a physical barrier to trade. In 1712 the River Douglas was surveyed by Thomas Steers with a view to making it navigable from Wigan to the Ribble and thereby opening up both the Preston area and, via coastal sailing vessels, Liverpool, to coal and other goods from the Wigan area.

The following year a bill was presented to make the Douglas navigable, but was rejected. A further bill was submitted and, after heated argument, finally passed in 1720. Amongst arguments against the Bill [38] were that it would destroy several thousand acres of rich meadow land which provided hay as winter feed for a great number of cattle, and that the Bill was for private gain and not to the public good. Arguments for the Bill, all of which were countered to a greater or lesser extent, included: that it would save considerable carriage on coal; that it would make the transportation of lime easier; that all sorts of merchandise could be brought up to Wigan; that the dangers of crossing the river at fords would be lessened; that it would provide employment both for boatmen and for poor labourers employed in its construction; and that the highways on the deep clay were deeply rutted and nearly impassable in a wet season and were a great expense to the landowners. This latter argument was countered by the statement that it was the custom in this part of

Parbold Hall, showing an apparently older three-storey east side and newer two-storey west side.

the county to carry most of the goods on horseback, the causeways being generally well paved. Indeed, it was argued that the navigation was likely to create a worse situation, since most of the coal had to be carted to the loading point and the roads near to the navigation would thus become even worse. The submission concerning the customary use of packhorses is supported, indirectly, by the will of Thomas Lancaster, carrier, of Parbold, who left his gang of twenty-one packhorses and saddles to his son in 1763.[39]

An estimate [40] of the charges for the work made in 1733 put the price at £6,684 13*s*. The specification included making 'a depth of water of one yard and a width of five yards in spring tides' to a lock near Rufford, providing for locks of twelve feet wide and sixty feet long between the gates, and continuing the walls for fifteen feet below the lower gates and twelve feet above the upper gates. There was to be a total of ten locks, including one at Newburgh Mill (possibly close to Douglas Mill), one near the Douglas Chapel, and one at the end of the long cut near a sharp bend, which can be identified as being near Gillibrands. Indeed, Lock Meadow and the old lock are shown on the Gillibrand estate map of about 1809. The quotation included building locks, raising bridge arches and so on, the typical price for a lock being £386. The bulk of the work was carried out after 1737, and the actual cost incurred between then and 1767 on making the canal navigable was over £32,000.[41]

Detailed accounts [42] of the building work give further information concerning construction and materials. For instance, an item for 'getting stone' for two locks above Deans suggests that the locks were walled in stone rather than being of turf; as does the payment for 'masons work at Dean Locks.' Similarly, an item 'for flagging at Gillibrands Lock' gives an indication of the finishing around the lock areas. A considerable amount of timber was required, which was obtained from several places in the area, including Parbold;[43] local quarries probably supplied the stone; and, although no details have been found, the work must have provided considerable employment for local men. In the accounts, the phrase 'gave him to drink two shillings and six pence' seems to accompany nearly every payment, and would suggest that this perk, a very generous one in relation to money values at that time, was part of the accepted practice.

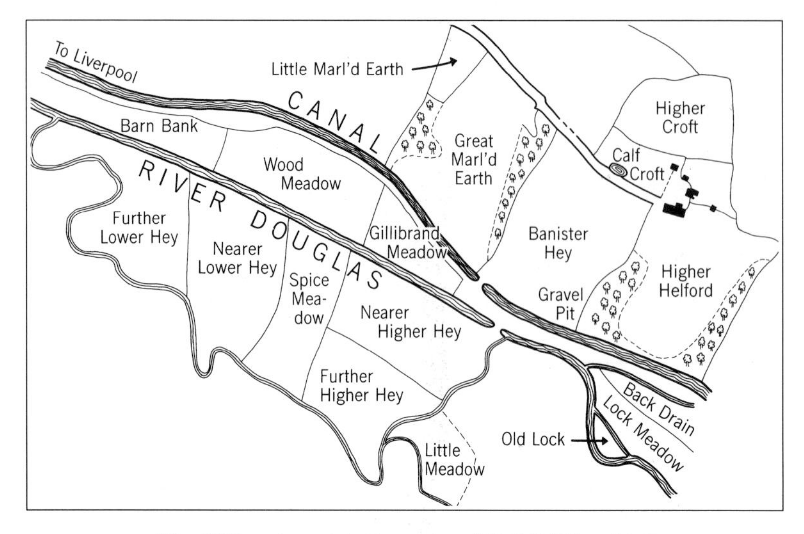

The Gillibrand estate in about 1809. (LRO DDSc 126/36)

Construction of the canal necessitated the acquisition of land. Land purchased from Mr Jonathan Gillibrand in Parbold in 1738 amounted to two rods, ten poles and two perches, for which the sum of £34 7*s*. 6*d*. was paid.[44]

The Douglas was finally declared fit for navigation in 1742, thirty years after the original survey had been carried out, and records survive of a number of the vessels which operated upon it. It seems probable that between Wigan and about Parbold the boats were 'bow hauled', that is pulled by teams of men walking along the bank or tow path, but from about Parbold to the sea they were actually sailed. Indeed, some appear to have been sea-going, proceeding around the coast to Liverpool.

The success of the early, mainly river navigations, led to the realisation that canals would be a valuable means of transport, and to a flurry of canal building. The politics and machinations behind the building of the Leeds and Liverpool Canal are outside the scope of our story, but they were considerable. The first length of the canal, from Newburgh to Liverpool, was opened in 1771, but this created a problem of water supply, since the canal company was not allowed to take water from the Douglas. Work had been proceeding on a cut, known as Leigh's Cut, to bypass the river below Gathurst, and the canal company now proceeded to take

Parbold Graving Dock.

over Leigh's Cut and, subsequently, the Douglas Navigation. The canal company then started work to complete Leigh's Cut and by 1774 the canal was navigable from Liverpool to Newburgh, via Leigh's Cut to Gathurst, and up the Douglas to Wigan.

The original plan was for the main line to head north from Parbold towards Mawdesley, bypassing Wigan, and to this end a short stub cut towards Mawdesley was made at Parbold. This route was later abandoned, but the original cut subsequently became Parbold graving dock, and is clearly visible today. The amount of work which had to be carried out was considerable, and to achieve it a large workforce would have been required. Unfortunately, there again appears to be no information concerning the size of the local workforce which was employed, nor where migrant workers came from and the impact they had upon the locality; one can assume that this must have been considerable, and it would be interesting to know what local reaction was and what the relations were like between the locals and the 'navigators' and their hangers-on.

The opening of the canal was an important step in promoting the economic development of the Parbold area. It provided a ready means of transporting the area's products, especially coal and stone, as well as allowing the opportunity to bring corn into the area for milling, manure and lime for the land and general goods such as groceries and so on. Associated with this trade was the establishment of stockyards and wharves, traces of which still remain in some instances. On the canal at Gillibrands there was a wharf for stone, which was connected with the quarries by a railway system which remained operational until well into this century, and which was itself probably preceded by a tramway system. Nearby was a dock which was probably associated with the late eighteenth-century Gillibrand colliery, and there was also a coal wharf at Owler Lane, while evidence of more general trade remains at the mill farm shop, where a lifting beam into a warehouse can still be seen.

The canal provided employment both to those people who worked on the boats and to those who worked at the graving dock. Boat building is recorded in Parbold [45] as early as 1786, when a boat of 47 tons built by Anthony Cartmel, shipwright, was launched. The tithe map shows the Saw Pit boatyard near the mill farm shop being run by one William Cartmel in 1837, which would suggest that this vessel was built there rather than in Newburgh. Boats with a total tonnage of 143 tons are also recorded as being built in Parbold between 1773 and 1781, and it would seem likely that these were built at the Parbold graving dock.

In addition to carrying freight, the canal also carried passengers on the so-called 'fly boats', which offered an express service between Wigan and Liverpool. The service left Liverpool at eight in the morning and arrived in Wigan at five in the afteroon. The fare to Owler's Lane (Alder Lane) Parbold, was 3*s.* 6*d.* in the front cabin and 2*s.* 4*d.* in the back cabin—very considerable sums. The present-day Spar shop was at that time a stable for the horses which towed the barges, and the grooves etched by the tow ropes into the stones under the bridges are lasting reminders of the labour of horses on the canal.

THE RAILWAY

The great expansion in the development of railways which took place throughout the country in the 1840s and 1850s continued the opening up of the Parbold area which had been begun by the

Douglas Navigation, and which had gained momentum with the building of the Leeds and Liverpool Canal. With the coming of the railway, came the beginnings of the canal's hundred-year period of decline. The Douglas Valley provided the natural route for the railway between Manchester and the coast at Southport and, with the completion and opening of the line on 9 April 1845, Parbold became accessible as a commuter area for the better-off. At the same time it became available as a recreational area to the less well-off from the Manchester conurbation, a use which was to reach a peak in the 1930s.

The building of the railway must have had similar social consequences as did the cutting of the canal, with a large influx of migrant workers into the village. To what extent the building phase provided employment for local people is not evident, but when the railway was opened it provided a small amount of direct local employment, which can be identified from the census returns for 1861 onwards.

A survey carried out in 1845 has provided us with a detailed plan of the land adjacent to the proposed line of the railway,[46] and part of this survey is shown for the Gillibrands area. The schedule drawn up to accompany the map at the time of the survey gives details of the owners, lessees or occupiers, and descriptions of the numbered plots.

To accommodate the economic activity of the village, sidings

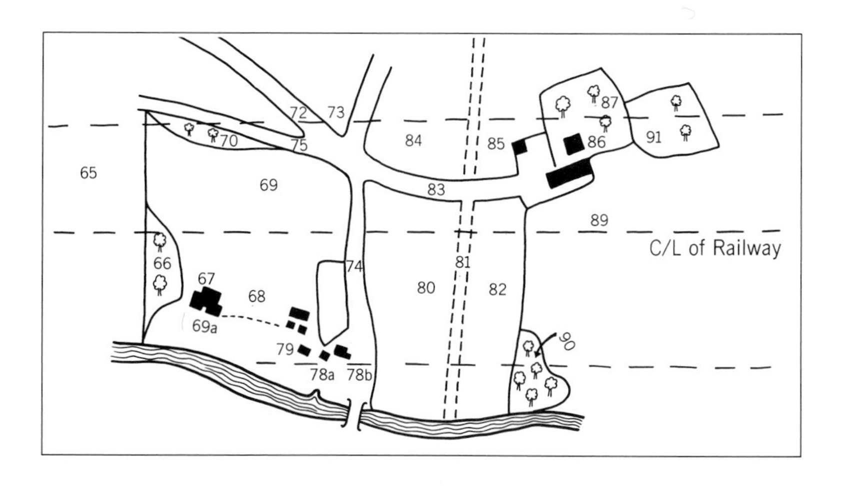

Extract from the survey for the building of the railway, 1845, showing the Gillibrands area. (LRO PR 503)

were established below the quarry on Parbold Hill, by Parbold brickworks, and immediately to the east of the station, where there was a coal yard and where general goods were handled. As has been noted earlier, some railway papers for 1870 refer to the station as 'Newburgh station'.[47] Although no attempt has been made here to investigate the history of the railway in detail, some indication of traffic and goods handled can be seen from cash receipts which show as customers Platt and Co., Platt and Magnall, H. & R. Ainscough and Winnards. A delivery note to the Leeds and Yorkshire Railway from Platt and Magnall for 1868 is for bricks to Southport; and telegraphic messages for 1878 refer to wagons left at both Barton's siding and Platt's siding.

19-CENTURY DEVELOPMENT

The earliest detailed map we have of Parbold is a map of the estates of Mary and Elizabeth Tyrell dated 1786.[48] The Misses Tyrell were the heirs to Thomas Crisp, whose daughter married Sir John Tyrell and subsequently gave birth to two daughters, who inherited the Parbold estate. Although the map shows only their land, it covers the majority of Parbold and the main areas of population can be identified, but it can be seen that there was no real concentration of population, and that Parbold was made up of a number of relatively scattered hamlets. There was a hamlet centered around the Stocks Tavern area and extending along Mill Lane and Bradshaw Lane; another cluster of houses at Newcotts Fold; others in Tanhouse Lane, Lancaster Lane and at isolated sites on the common and elsewhere. The Gillibrands estate is not shown on this map, being in separate ownership, but is shown in detail on a separate estate map of 1809.

The large-scale tithe map of 1837 and the 6-inch Ordnance Survey map of 1845 give the most detailed picture of the village yet, but in essence show little change from the earlier map, apart from a slightly increased housing density along Mill Lane.

The railway came to Parbold in 1855, and by the time that the 25-inch Ordnance Survey map was published, in 1893, the village had almost assumed the appearance which existed up to the rash of development in the 1960s. Station Road had been developed, and

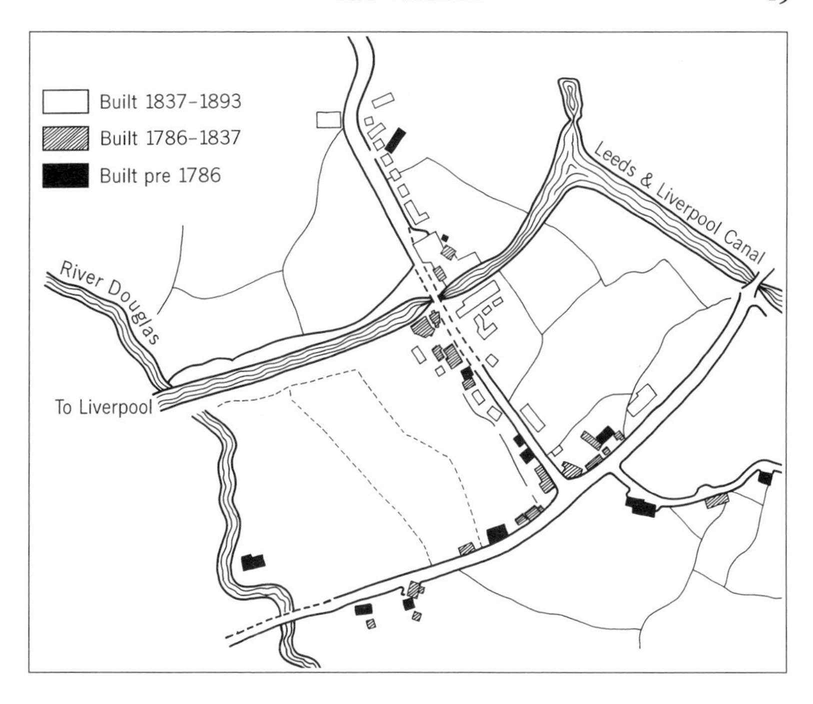

Development of Parbold centre (1786–1893)

The Old Mill Farm Shop, formerly a canal side warehouse. Entrances on three levels and a lifting beam remain.

Mid-nineteenth-century houses in Station Road.

the *Railway Hotel* built, both the new Church of England and Catholic churches were built, and industrialisation took the form of the brickworks on Alder Lane, and the new corn mill which had replaced the windmill.

2

The People

POPULATION

The first indication of population can be obtained from the Hearth Tax returns [49] for Lady Day 1666. This tax, which was first raised in 1662, had to be paid by all householders except those in receipt of poor relief, or living in houses valued at less than twenty shillings per year. The village constable was charged with compiling a list of householders, together with the number of hearths in each household, the list being submitted to the justices at the quarter sessions. Many of these lists have survived throughout the country and provide not only a list of the population but also an indication of the relative size of the houses in which they lived. The list for Parbold gives fifty hearths counted in twenty-seven households.

The figure of twenty-seven houses agrees very well with the total of twenty-four dwellings identified in 1623. Using the commonly used factor of 4.5 persons per household, this would give an approximate population for the village of one hundred and twenty persons.

The taking of a regular census on a ten-yearly cycle began in 1801, the information for the period up to 1891 being summarised as follows:

Year	*Population*	*Households*	*Average Households*
1801	255		
1811	348		
1821	339	69	4.91
1831	382		
1841	418		
1851	473	87	5.44

Year	*Population*	*Households*	*Average Households*
1861	474	92	5.15
1871	477	89	5.40
1881	529	97	5.45
1891	598		

The average size of household in the nineteenth century appears to have been considerably larger than the assumed average for the seventeenth. However, even taking an average of 5.4 would imply a population for 1666 of less than one hundred and fifty.

THE PARISH REGISTER

Parish registers were first ordered to be kept by Thomas Cromwell in 1538, the minister of the parish being required to keep in a book details of every baptism, wedding and burial at which he had officiated. The earliest surviving register for the parish of Eccleston is that for 1603. The Eccleston registers up to 1694 have been transcribed and published by the Lancashire Parish Register Society.[50]

Eccleston Church. The mother church for the parish including Parbold.

The baptisms and burials usually state not only the father's name, but also the township from which he came. The weddings sometimes state the township, but not always, or occasionally, 'of this parish'. This could mean from any of the four townships of the parish. Parbold entries are fairly common, and give a reasonable number of common Parbold names such as Lancaster, Lathom and Barton.

The first register shows very few entries for Douglas Chapel. Only twelve baptisms and four burials are recorded between 1603 and 1694. One of the burials is of Robert Walk, described as a 'Scotchman'. On 24 March 1660, Edward, the son of Jonathan Gellibrand of Parbold was baptised at Douglas Chapel. Jonathan Gellibrand was Rector of Eccleston.

The residents of Parbold, as parishioners of Eccleston, had the right of interment at Eccleston Church. The journey from Parbold to Eccleston over poor roads must have been quite difficult, but the registers would suggest that most of the burials took place there. A plan drawn up by Henry Sephton in 1716 [51] gives the names of those who were known to have been buried there as follows:

Within the Church	*In the Burial Ground*
Thomas Barton	John Bamber
Henry Fisher	Richard Bamber
John Gilyburn	John Fisher
James Howet	Henry Letham
William Howet	Thomas Letham
Thomas Lancaster	Richard Lancaster
William Letham	Thomas Lancaster
James Scolfield	Richard Rigby
Robert Willson	Henry Smallshaw
	William Willson

This list is made up almost entirely of well-known Parbold family names, which may suggest that only those who were better off were interred at Eccleston, but that in turn raises the question as to where the majority of ordinary people were buried. Certainly the list above is not complete. A number of wills, such as that of Arthur Finch,

1636,[52] specify that they are to be buried at the parish church of Eccleston.

PARBOLD FAMILIES

The census returns available for public inspection from 1841 to 1891 give a complete list of the inhabitants at ten-yearly intervals. Before 1841 there are a number of sources which give incomplete lists, but which enable the main families which have lived in the village for generations to be identified, and which provide a valuable genealogical source. The majority of these lists were compiled for taxation purposes, and include the Hearth Tax, Land Tax and taxes raised under the Poor Law. In the nineteenth century the publication of directories became popular and provides an additional source of information.

The Hearth Tax nominal roll for Parbold on Ladyday 1666 [53] provides the following information:

Jo. Crisp		Joh. Wilson	4
?	6	Henry Lathom	1
Tho. Hawett	3	Jo. Wakefield	2
Ja. Rigbye	2	Bryan ?	1
Wm. Lathome	1	Jonath. Jollybrand	4
Wm. Rigbye	2	Raph Nelson	2
Tho. Lathom	1	Brighowse	
John Stanford	1	Richard Lancaster	1
? Smallshawe	2	Raph Woodcock	1
Richard Durneinge	3	Hugh Wilson	1
Wm. Hawett jun.	1	Richard Hawett	1
Rich. Paterick	2	Wm. Wilson	1
Jo. Barton	2	Douglas ?	1
Widow Barton	2		

Well-known Parbold names appear on this list, and it is possible to speculate, with a greater or lesser degree of accuracy, on the location of their dwellings. John Crisp, for example, we know was at Parbold

Hall. Gillibrand House is readily identifiable as the residence of Jonath. Jollybrand, and Lancaster House in Lancaster Lane and Lathom House in Lathom Avenue would seem probable locations for these respective families. However, reference to the 1845 six-inch Ordnance Survey map would throw this latter conclusion into doubt, since this map gives the present-day Lathom House as 'Barton's'. Smallshaw's Farm is still known by that name, but strictly speaking is in Wrightington, whilst the present-day Woodcock Hall is definitely in Newburgh. (But the Parbold Woodcocks are possibly a separate family from those in Newburgh.) Hawett Hill would seem to owe its designation to the family of that name. These names crop up repeatedly in the story of the village.

In October 1751 the justices at Wigan quarter sessions requested Thomas Hawkeshead of Heskin and Richard Prescott of Dalton to carry out a survey and estimate of the yearly value of the messuages, tenements and heridatements in Parbold [54] and to report back at the next quarter sessions. The survey was required in order that the officers of the township could make a rate for the relief of the poor. The survey was reported back on 21 January 1752,[54] and accounted for 468 acres of land at a total value of just over £606. Thirty-one individuals were named. The details were as follows:

	A	R	P	£	*s.*	*d.*
Thomas Crisp Esq. for his Demesne land	141	2	2	141	3	6
Nicholas Rigby	16	1	–	19	3	6
The Rector of Eccleston for his tythes	"	"	"	30	"	"
Mr Gillibrand	26	1	"	38	"	"
Mr Spencer	3	"	1	5	2	0
Mr Nelson	6	2	"	9	9	9
Joseph Ashton	29	2	"	29	2	"
Mr Edward Fisher	14	"	"	14	7	"
Edward Woodcock for Crook Fields	10	"	"	11	13	"
Widow Lancaster for all	38	"	20	52	13	"
Thomas Lancaster	12	2	–	17	10	"
John Barton	9	"	"	13	"	"
Richard Nelson	7	1	"	9	9	6

	A	R	P	£	s.	d.
Evan Crookhall	3	1	20	4	18	"
and for part of Bartons	6	1	"	6	6	"
Thomas Barton	20	2	"	25	13	"
James Barton	4	1	"	7	15	"
James Bradshaw for Wakefields	16	"	20	17	8	6
do. for Chapple House	4	2	"	6	1	6
do. for Drapers	"	"	20	1	12	6
do. for old Lancasters, now John Heyes	2	"	30	3	15	"
Mr Causey for Heskin House	2	3	"	4	11	"
do. for School House	4	2	"	6	8	"
George Plumb	10	3	30	14	15	"
Richard Whitehead for Hawetts	11	3	"	13	7	"
Mr William Edden	10	2	"	14	7	6
and for Hardmans	1	1	"	2	15	"
Richard Hawett	11	"	20	10	3	6
do. for Haltons and Sought	13	2	20	13	8	"
Peter Law	4	3	"	7	18	6
do. for Common Close	2	"	"	2	"	"
do. for his cottage	"	2	"	1	5	"
James Standfield	2	1	"	4	5	"
John Bentham	1	2	20	3	10	"
Thomas Marsden	10	3	20	10	2	"
Thomas Edden	2	2	"	4	10	"
Douglas Mill	"	"	"	8	0	0
Jane Wilson	2	1	"	4	8	"
Widow Woodcock	1	3	"	3	3	"
Widow Hawet	1	2	30	4	2	6
Widow Ashton	"	3	"	2	"	"
Parbold Stone Delf	"	"	"	4	"	"
	468	2	30	606	11	6

In addition to the thirty-one individuals named, it is worth noting the two industrial activities recorded, namely Douglas Mill—the water mill—and the stone quarry on Parbold Hill. Perhaps the most interesting fact, however, is that of the fifteen family names given in the Hearth Tax returns, ten are represented in this list nearly a hundred years later.

A Land Tax was collected from 1692 until 1831, the usual rate being four shillings in the pound. Parbold was assessed to yield £31 10*s*. After 1780 the returns were sent to the clerk of the quarter sessions, and, with some exceptions like 1799, the records for Parbold are reasonably complete from 1781. They show the owners, occupiers and value of lands taxed. Although different combinations of lands under the same ownership may confuse the picture from year to year, properties with distinctive values, such as Gillibrands, assessed at £1 17*s*. 7*d*. in most years, may be readily identifiable even when under different ownerships. The returns are also useful in looking at different land uses, such as quarrying and mining, as well as indicating the principal inhabitants over the fifty-year period before the tithe map, and census returns provide similar but more detailed information. An example of a Land Tax return is shown.[55]

THE LANDOWNERS

The early history of the ownership of the manor of Parbold seems to be somewhat confused, and there are a number of slightly conflicting accounts. However, a general picture emerges as follows. In the latter part of the twelfth century Bernard of Parbold was the lord of the manor. It is thought that he was a younger son of Henry, son of Siward, lord of Lathom.[56] Bernard was succeeded by his son Henry, who was a benefactor of Burscough Priory, but who probably had no children, and the manor reverted to the ownership of the lordship of Lathom. Before 1242 Parbold was in the hands of Robert de Lathom, who passed it to his son Richard who had four daughters but no sons. Two of the daughters were childless, but in 1351 Parbold was claimed by descendants of two of the daughters, as well as by the Lathoms of Tarbock, another off-shoot of the Lathom family. The dispute was resolved by the manor once again being recovered by the head of the Lathom family, this time Sir Thomas de Lathom. He granted the manor to his younger son, Edward Lathom. Sir Thomas de Lathom's elder son, also Thomas, was the

An Assessment made in pursuance of an Act of Parliament passed in the 22 Year of his present Majesty's Reign for granting an Aid to his said Majesty by a Land Tax to be raised in Great Britain for the Service of the year 1782

Names of Proprietors	Names of Occupiers	Sums assessed £	s	d
Late Sr Jon. Sgvcels Heirs	The Revd Mr Walker	7	16	
Do for Parbold Quarry	Sundry Undertakers	..	4	..
Do for the Coal Pits	Wm Hen. & Thos Whittle	..	16	4
Mrs Rigbye	James Smith	1	..	..
Mrs Nelson	Mrs Nelson & Enoch Ellison	..		
Do for the Knotts	Enoch Ellison			
Do for Lancaster's	Thomas Leptrot	2	15	..
The Revd Mr Whitehead	Thos Glover for the Tithes	1	12	8
John Woodcock Esq	John Woodcock Esq	..	5	4
Mrs Sale	John Christopher	2	..	..
Mr Jos Ashton	Thomas Bullen	1	10	8
Late Mr Latham's Trustees	Do	..	12	..
Mr Mort	John Pennington	..	14	8
Mr Hatton	Mr Hatton	1	6	8
Do for Bentham's	Peter Livesey	..	3	..
James Bradshaw	James Bradshaw	..	3	4
Do for Chapell House &c	Richd Livesey	..	7	..
Do for Hawets	Robert Welch	..	13	4
Do for the Parrick	James Bradshaw	..	..	6
George Plumbe	George Plumbe	..	14	8
Thomas Glover	Thomas Glover	1	7	4
James Mawdesley	James Mawdesley	..	17	6
John Scarisbrick	James Woods	..	12	..
Richard Clayton	John Fisher & others	..	6	..
Susan Barton	Susan Barton	..	8	4
Thomas Eden	Thomas Eden	..	18	..
Do for Hardman House	Thomas Dicconson Junr	..	2	8
Edward Heaton	William Ashcroft	..	5	4
Do for Common Close	Henry Fazakerley	..	2	..
James Culshaw	Alexander Roper	..	8	..
Edward Bickerstaff	Edward Seddon & others	..	1	..

Extract from the Parbold Land Tax return, 1782

line from which the Earls of Derby descended. The Lathom family tree has been drawn up by Berry.[57] Edward Lathom was further endowed by his elder brother with part of the manor of Wrightington, and his grandson, another Edward, added further to the family lands by acquiring the manor of Allerton during the fifteenth century. The Lathoms of Parbold thus became lords of both Parbold and Allerton and remained so until the family's demise at the end of the seventeenth century.

Following the Reformation the Lathoms remained adherents to the old faith and were one of the prominent Lancashire Catholic families. A will of 1623 [58] provides an insight into religious tensions of the time. Thomas Legh of Hallam bequeathed £50 to his nephew, Thomas Lathom, and £20 to Douglas Chapel by Parbold, praying the 'good old parson of Standish, my old maister & the parson of Ecleston to do their best to roote out popery'. A generation before, Edward Legh of Hallam had bequeathed '. . . unto my nephwe Lathom of Parbold my Rapier and dagger desiringe him & his bedfellowe to honor god with prayers and thanksgeuinge daylie in theire house at Parbold and in so doinge god will bless them . . . both in theire house & in the feilds.' [59]

The historical ownership of land determines the most likely places to search for documents which provide the basis for investigating the history of the area. In Parbold the most important landholding, that of the manor itself, passed from the Lathoms to John Crisp after the Civil Wars. John Crisp's descendant, Thomas Crisp, became Member of Parliament for Ilchester in Somerset in 1727. He died in 1758 leaving a widow, a daughter, but no sons. His daughter, Mary, married Sir John Tyrell of Herne in the county of Essex, by whom she had two daughters, Mary and Elizabeth, and the estate in Parbold eventually passed to them. The formal passing of the estate to Sir John and Mary Tyrell is recognised in a concord of August 1752.[60] At that time the estate was detailed as 82 messuages, one water corn mill, 84 gardens, 64 orchards, 200 acres of ploughed

Two versions of the arms of the Lathoms of Parbold.
1. Described as: *Or, on a chief indented, azure, three plates, over all a bendlet, gules.*
2. Described as: *Or on a chief indented azure three plates.*

land, 200 acres of meadow, 400 acres of pasture and 300 acres of woodland. An estate map, made in 1786, shows in detail the Misses Tyrell's land in Parbold. In 1790 the estate, including land in Wrightington, Newburgh and Dalton, as well as Parbold, and totalling 1,256 acres, was advertised for sale [61] at Christie's in Pall Mall. The estate was acquired by William Dicconson for £34,260 15*s.* 9*d.* To raise the money it was necessary to sell or mortgage land in Lincoln, Wigan, Penwortham, Coppull, Charnock Richard, Croston, Worthington, Burscough and Dalton, and an Act of Parliament was needed. At this time William Dicconson was 63 years old, and his wife, Meliora, over 75. They had no direct descendants, and the estate eventually passed to his brother, Edward. As we have seen, the estates subsequently passed to Charles Scarisbrick. Not only was he extremely rich, but he was also a very unusual man. He lived at Scarisbrick Hall, and was responsible for engaging Pugin to remodel the hall. He seems to have been 'a source of puzzlement' to everyone at Stonyhurst School and little understood by his contemporaries.[62]

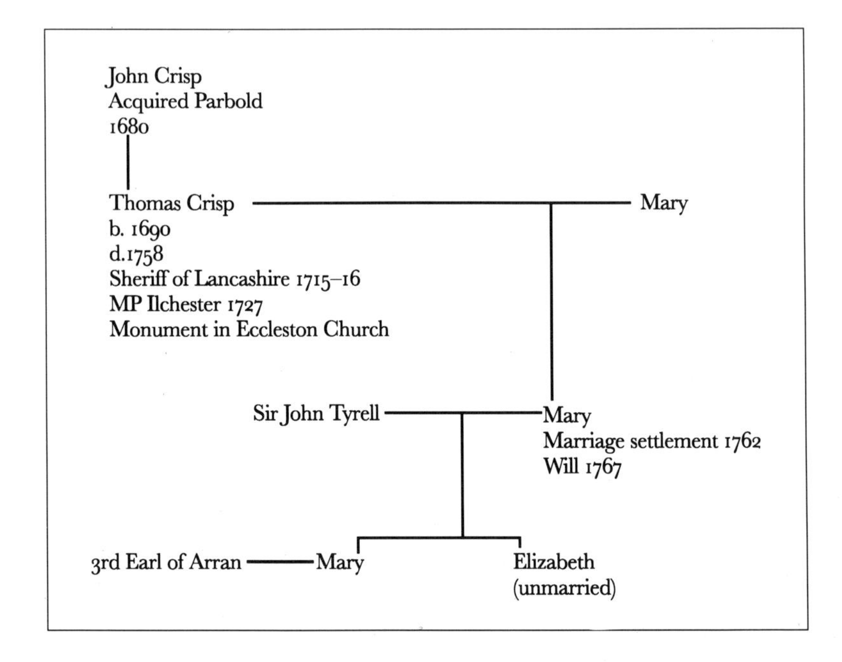

The Crisps and Tyrells—Lords of the Manor of Parbold 1680–1791.

He was from a Catholic family, but never married. However, he had a long-term relationship with his German mistress, by whom he had several children. Although an absentee landlord, the estate papers suggest that he took a fairly active interest in his estate.

The origins of the Gillibrands estate are shrouded in mystery, but it seems always to have been separate from the manor. It was of some 28 acres or so, and after the death of Jonathan Gillibrand in 1759 the estate was left to Martha Sale, the wife of William Sale of Leigh.[62] It subsequently became incorporated in the Parbold estate in about 1800.

The Hesketh of Rufford held land in Parbold from early times. The lands which had been held by the Knights of St John seem to have been taken over by Lord Derby following the Dissolution. Other minor land holdings included Bispham School, the land being acquired by the will of Richard Durning in 1692. Fairhurst Hall was an important landholding in the area, and was situated right on the township boundary. Indeed, the boundary seems to have passed through the house area, as the house itself was technically in Wrightington, while some of the outbuildings were in Parbold. The estate held some acres in Parbold.

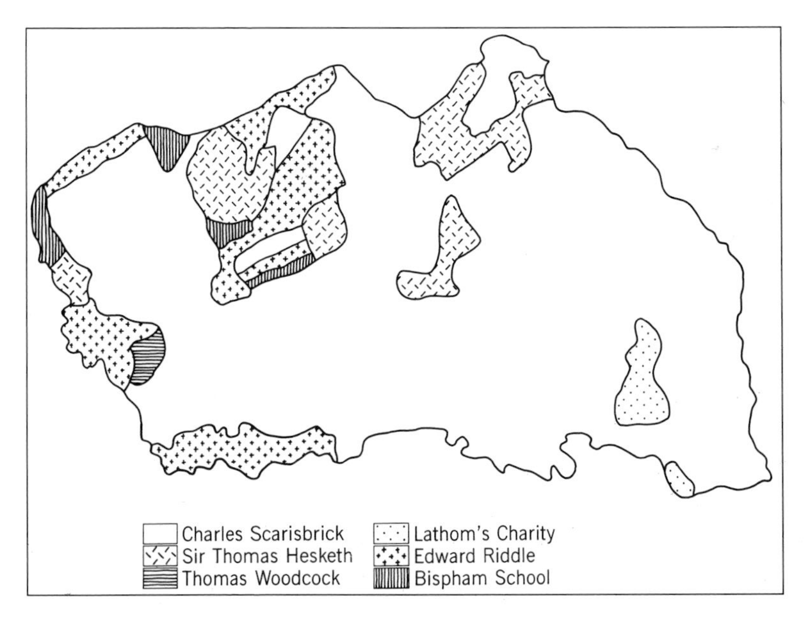

Landowners, 1837.

The evidence from the land tax returns on land ownership is confusing, but suggests a wider base of land ownership. For example, the land tax returns for both 1782 and 1797 show nearly 30 landowners. It would seem probable that these are not true land holders but tenants in some instances. At any rate, by the time of the tithe survey in 1837 there were only six landowners, all of whom were absentees, although all living fairly close by.

Numerous leases survive which illustrate the way in which land was tenanted. This was either for a fixed term or for 'three lives'. Delf House in the Fairy Glen, for example, was leased to William Halton in 1803 [63] for eleven years at £75 *per annum*. Various restrictions were placed upon the leaseholder, including the compulsion to have corn ground at the landowner's mill at the usual rates, the necessity to keep a cock and a dog for the landlord's use, not to grow potatoes for sale, not to break up meadow ground or more than six acres of pasture in any one year, to bring back one cart load of dung for every load of wheat, straw or clover hay taken off the property, and the obligation to perform court duties for the property at the manor courts. In 1814 the lease was renewed for £150,[64] but by 1842 the rental had been reduced to £126 when the farm was rented to Thomas and Joseph Speakman,[65] and had

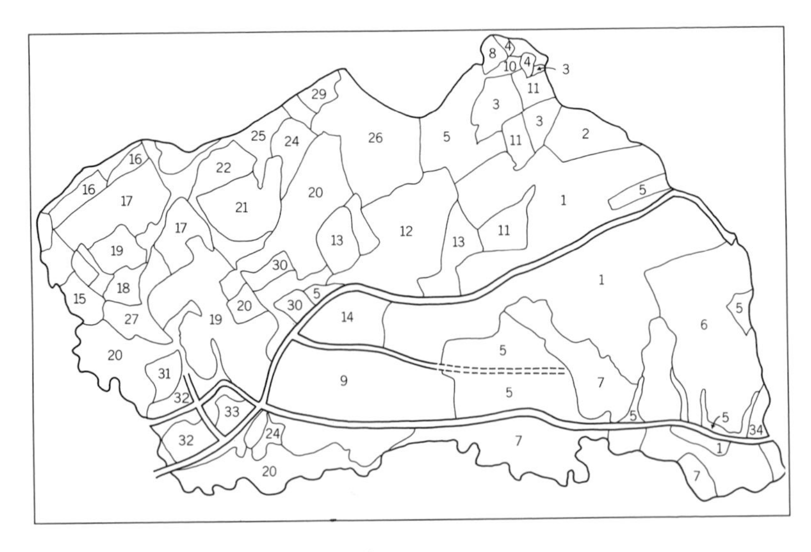

Land occupiers, 1837.

further been reduced to £108 in 1851, when the tenant was Thomas Speakman the Younger.[66]

The system of leasing for lives involved the leasing of a property until the last of the individuals nominated in the lease had died. This type of lease provided a high degree of security of tenure over a fairly long period, particularly if fairly young individuals were nominated, as was the case with the property leased by Mary Crisp to William Willson, a carpenter. William Willson was 41, but the other lives nominated were Edward, son of Richard Willson, aged twelve, and Thomas Finch, aged eleven. Frequently, leases for lives involved not only a rent, but also payment by service, or 'boon'. For instance, William Willson contracted to pay a boon of one day's reaping or a payment of eight pence.[67]

Landowners and occupiers, 1837

Number	*Occupier*	*Owner*
1	Wm. Widdows	Charles Scarisbrick
2	Henry Dicconson	Charles Scarisbrick
3	Henry Blundell	Charles Scarisbrick
4	David Dicconson	Charles Scarisbrick
5	John Ainscough	Sir Thomas Hesketh
6	William Hatton	Charles Scarisbrick
7	Barton and Cookson	Charles Scarisbrick
		Lathom's Charity
8	Thomas Morrow	Charles Scarisbrick
9	John Greener	Charles Scarisbrick
10	Robert Welsch	Charles Scarisbrick
11	William Martland	Sir Thomas Hesketh
12	Richard Swift	Charles Scarisbrick
13	John Swift	Sir Thomas Hesketh
14	James Robinson	Charles Scarisbrick
15	John Barton	Sir Thomas Hesketh
16	Margaret Blackburn	Edward Riddle

17	Anne Welsch	Charles Scarisbrick
18	John Barton	Charles Scarisbrick
19	William Liptrot	?
20	Richard Hunter	Edward Riddle
21	Richard Martland Jnr.	Sir Thomas Hesketh
22	James Robinson	Sir Thomas Hesketh
23		
24	Richard Smith	Charles Scarisbrick
25	Margaret Blackburn	Edward Riddle
26	Thomas Platt	Charles Scarisbrick
27	James Whalley	Charles Scarisbrick
28	Edward Langton	Edward Riddle
29	John Parr	Edward Riddle
30	John Mason	Charles Scarisbrick
31	James Taylor	Thomas Woodcock
32	William Cartmel	Charles Scarisbrick
33	Henry Clayton	Charles Scarisbrick
34	William Richardson	Charles Scarisbrick
35	John Culshaw	Bispham School
36	Thomas Shorrock	Bispham School
S	Charles Scarisbrick	Charles Scarisbrick

THE POOR

Poverty was an ever-present problem, which may in part have been alleviated by the monastic establishments until their dissolution in the sixteenth century. Matters may not have improved greatly until, by the Poor Law Act of 1601, overseers of the poor were appointed each year in each parish or township from among the more substantial householders. It was their duty to maintain the poor and set them to work if possible. Funds were to be provided by a local tax, and it was also the overseer's responsibility to collect this money, which was to be used to provide for the old, the sick, or others who were unable to work.

This system remained in force until the mid-nineteenth century, when parishes were united into Poor Law Unions to provide for the poor. The dependency of the poor on the parish gives rise to the expression 'going on the parish'. However, because paupers were on parish funds there was a reluctance to allow potential paupers to move into the parish from elsewhere and settle. This situation was formally recognised by the Act of Settlement 1662, which empowered the overseers of the poor to remove a stranger from the parish within forty days if he or she had no prospect of work or if he did not rent property worth £10 per year. A stranger coming into the district temporarily had to bring a certificate from his home parish guaranteeing to take him back if he was liable to become a charge upon the parish.

Much of the work of the quarter sessions was concerned with dealing with the administration of this law and disputes arising from it, of which there are several documented cases concerning Parbold. The problem of not being saddled with the expense of maintaining the poor from other parishes is illustrated by the petition of the inhabitants of Wrightington and Parbold to the justices on 19 January 1679,[68] when they petitioned for the removal of a 'wandering woman being great with child' to Lathom, which is 'her last place of Lawful settlement and alsoe where she was gotten with child', since they were afraid of her being a burden to them. Society at that time was practical but not always compassionate.

The continual moving on of poor people is also shown by two court orders,[69, 70] for the removal of John Halton and his wife Jane in 1666 and 1667 from Dalton into the 'towne' of Parbold or Wrightington. After the first order the Haltons must have gone back to Dalton. The second order makes specific provision that if the inhabitants were to find themselves aggrieved and feel that they should not be settled in Parbold, then they should be heard at the next sessions giving notice to the inhabitants of the town where they intend to settle them a fortnight before the next sessions are due to be held. The Haltons were subsequently moved on to Wrightington.

About ten orders concerning settlements and removals survive

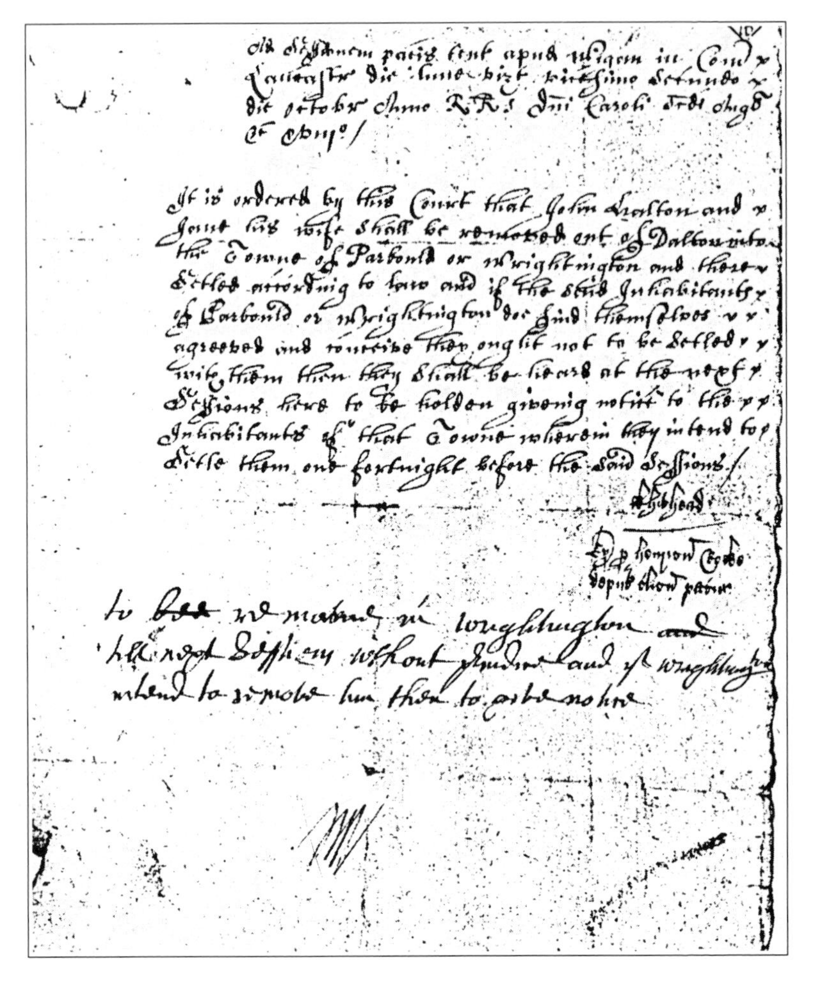

It is ordered by this Court that John Halton and Jane his wife shall be removed out of Dalton into the Towne of Parbold or Wrightington and there settled according to law and if the said Inhabitants of Parbold or Wrightington doe find themselves agreeved and conceive they ought not to be settled with them then they shall be heard at the next Sessions here to be holden giving notice to the Inhabitants of that Towne wherein they intend to settle them one fortnight before the said Sessions.

Settlement order for John Halton and Jane, his wife, 1667. (LRO QSP 315/10)

for Parbold covering the period from 1666 to 1714. A similar number of petitions for relief also survive. The petition of Richard Crosse, dated 1676, describes him as as 'an impotent person' with a wife and four children, and with an allowance of six pence a week towards their maintenance. The court ordered as follows:

> the overseers of the poore of Parbold shall fort[h]with uppon notice hereof pay & allow unto Richard Crosse a poore lame man the weekly summe of twelve pence for releefe of himselfe & Chilldren

> Or otherwise uppon Complaint made to any Justice of Peace . A warrant to bee awarded to take them bound to answer theire contempts att the next sessions here to bee holden.[71]

It appears that there was some disagreement over the treatment of Richard Crosse. The reverse side of this order bears some interesting figures:

> A True accoumpt of the monyes paid to Richard Crosse of parbold since his Leg was hurt as followeth by mee Richard moress overseer of the poore in Parbold;

about Easter 1673 John Stananought then overseer gave the said Richard Cross beeing newly hurt	0	10	0
In the yeare 1674 to Dockter barron towards his cure	0	10	0
& by weekly payments to the said Rich: Cross that yeare	5	05	9
the same yeare towards his cure	1	0	0
In 1675 in weekly payments	2	12	0
In this year 1676 paid		14	0
Sum totall	10	01	09

These figures appear to be a defence against this order and imply that Richard Crosse had been treated rather better by the overseers of the poor for Parbold than the petition would suggest. An interesting incidental from these figures is the use of the term 'Dockter' which seems a very early use of the term, and implies the recognition of someone in the village who occupied the position of some sort of primitive medical practitioner. Some ten years earlier, a Richard Crosse, who may or may not be the same person, having lived decently in Parbold for seven years, but now being without a house, applied successfully to the magistrates for permission to build a house.[72]

The name Crosse seems to have been an unfortunate one. A few years later, in 1714, complaint was made that William Crosse, together with his wife Alice and her son Thomas, had recently moved from Orrell to Parbold to gain a settlement there, but they were judged to be poor and the overseers in Parbold were required to remove them to Orrell, where the local overseers were required to relieve and provide for them.[73]

Poverty seems to have fairly frequently been a source of controversy. When John Leighe was injured in a marl pit, the quarter sessions sitting at Ormskirk made an order, on 11 July 1626, for a collection to be made for his relief, amounting to one whole fifteenth, which was to be paid to him towards 'the sustentacion, manetaynance and recoverie of his former strength'.[74] Accompanying this order in the records is a list of persons who refused to pay this tax.

Another matter coming before the magistrates was the question of the maintenance of bastard children. A typical petition dealt with by the magistrates was that of Margaret Winstanley of Orrell who swore that James Livesay of Parbold was the father of her bastard son, James. He was declared the putative father by the justices, and ordered to pay to the overseers of Orrell the yearly sum of £1 6*s*. 8*d*. in four equal instalments from the time of the birth until the child was fourteen. The overseers were to pay this over to Margaret Winstanley for maintenance, but the mother and father were required to indemnify Orrell township from all costs.[75]

An additional cause of hardship was the fines imposed upon religious recusants. Petitions citing two such instances survive from 1679 and 1680. The first [76] states:

> This is to certify all whom it may concerne that these persons whose names are subscribed beinge popish recusants inhabiting in Parbould in this County of Lancaster, are poore and needy and noe wayes able to pay the sessions fees neither did they pay our Clarke any thinge at their binding over, witnesse our hands this 13th day of October, Anno domini: 1679:
>
> Henery Woodcock
> James Lancaster
> Richard Draper
> Jenet patricke
> beinge four in number
>
> Edw. Chisenhale
> Hen. Stanington [77]

The second petition is signed by James Scofield, overseer of the poor in Parbold and John Chisenhall and William Banester, constables, and cites John Rigby, Nicholas Turner, Richard Corse and Richard Draper as poor recusants.

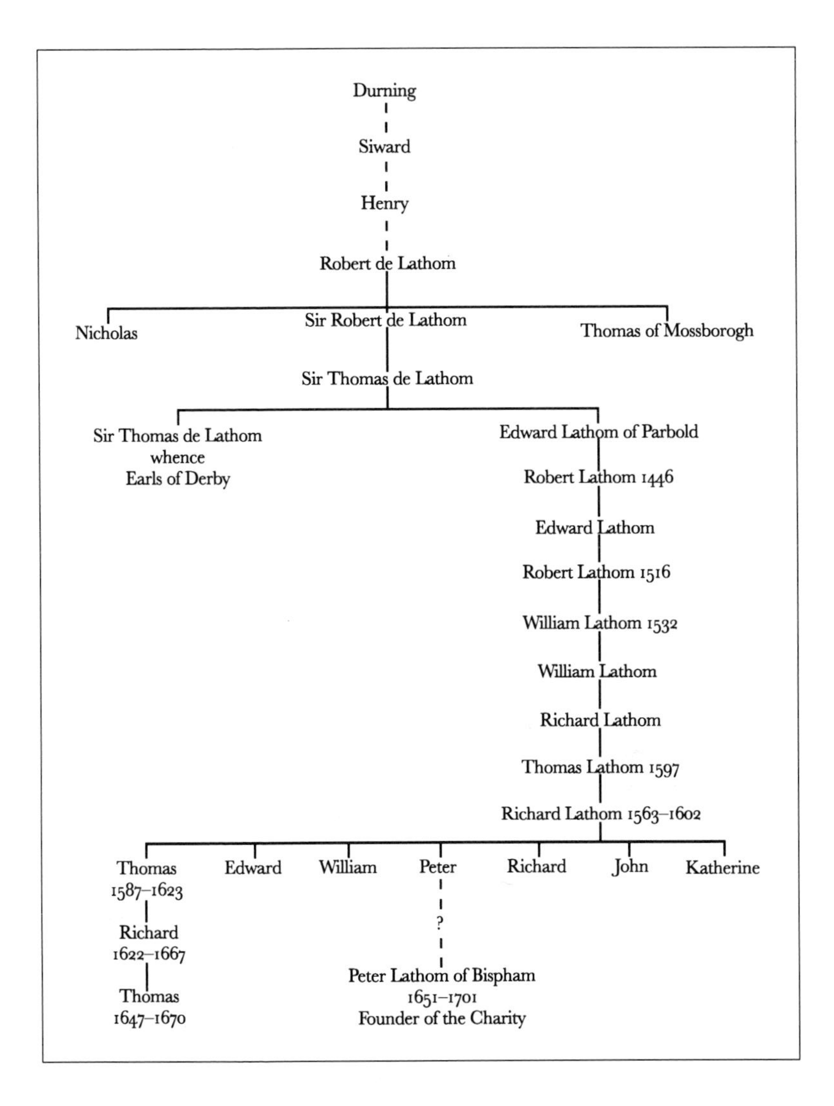

Genealogy of the Lathoms of Parbold and Peter Lathom, Founder of the Charity. (Based on R. J. A. Berry, Hist. Soc. Lancs and Ches. 97 1946, 85–100 and R. Stewart-Brown, 'A History of the Manor and Township of Allerton', Liverpool, 1911.)

CHARITY

A minor contribution to the alleviation of poverty was that which was provided by charity. Parbold was poorly endowed in this respect. The main charities having some impact on the villages were those established under the wills of Jonathan Gillibrand, Peter Lathom and Richard Durning.

Jonathan Gillibrand died in 1759, apparently without direct family. No relatives are mentioned in his short will, which provided for a dole of £10 to be paid to the poor on the day of his funeral. He also left money to Douglas Chapel, the interest to be paid to the curate, and left £20, on which the interest was to be paid to the curate at the chapel, provided he preached a sermon in the chapel on New Year's Day. £100 was also left to provide an income which was to be used to provide cloth for distribution to 'the poor and most necessitous people of Parbold' on New Year's Day immediately after Divine Service. The interest was to be divided into two parts, one to provide linen, the other to provide woollen cloth. Accounts for the charity are extant [78] for the period 1868 to 1903. They provide details of who received benefit, and in many instances how much they received. Numbers of recipients seem to have varied considerably from year to year. In 1868 there were 59 recipients, declining steadily until 1872, when there were 43. The following year the number dropped dramatically to sixteen. Numbers remained relatively low until the mid-eighties, when it suddenly shot up to over forty again. In 1885 the charity was worth £6 8*s*. 4*d*., which purchased 385 yards of cloth. This was distributed as nine handouts of five yards each and thirty of ten yards each.

Peter Lathom, who was described as 'of Bispham', was born about 1650 and died in 1701. He is a character about whom relatively little is known, although he has been extensively researched by one of his descendants.[58] The supposed connections between Peter Lathom and the Lathoms of Parbold remains unproven, although there is a fair amount of circumstantial evidence. Peter Lathom acquired land in several townships and parishes within the district, including Parbold, the charity lands being shown on the tithe map. In 1828 the rentals on the charity lands were the not inconsiderable sum of £339 10*s*., and these were distributed in seventeen townships in south-west Lancashire.

Richard Durning is best known for the setting up of Durning's School in Bispham, and will be discussed further in the section on education.

LIFE IN THE 17TH CENTURY

A number of wills and their associated inventories giving a list of the items forming the estate (described as 'goods, chattels and cattells') of the deceased survive from the seventeenth century, which enable a picture of the way of life of the people of Parbold of that time to be reconstructed. The names of the individuals, their occupations, if known, and the value of their estates are summarised below. They cover a range of the better-off inhabitants.

The majority of the testators were described as 'yeomen', but, not surprisingly in a rural community, even those not so described frequently left estates with cattle and crops figuring largely in it. These aspects will not be discussed here since they provide information on farming and will be considered in that context. In addition to this information, however, the inventories provide details of houses, household effects, personal items, luxuries and the general way of life.

The inventories were made by other members of the community who were considered competent to assess the value of the goods making up the estate. It is said that such inventories often significantly under-valued the estates, but even so the information is extremely interesting. Frequently, the items are listed room-by-room as the appraisers worked their way around the house, and the rooms in which the items were found can be identified, thereby giving an idea of what the house was like.

Thomas Patrick died in 1664. His estate was appraised by John Barton, Richard Durning, Richard Prescot and Robert Stopforth, and valued at £48 16*s*. 4*d*. From the inventory we can tell that his house included a parlour, a 'little house and lofte', a ground-floor chamber next to the parlour, a chamber next to the house, a buttery, a chamber over the buttery, and a stable. The term 'house' in this context means the living room, and is used in this way in a number

The first part of the will of Richard Lancaster, 1671. (LRO WCW 1672)

of the seventeenth-century Parbold wills. A chamber is, of course, a bedroom.

Richard Barton died the following year. His inventory also gives an opportunity to form some idea of his home. It comprised the chamber above the house, a little chamber, another little chamber, a downstair chamber and a buttery. Richard Barton's estate was valued at £73 4*s.* 10*d.*

Elizabeth Barton, a widow, who died at the turn of the century, in 1700, was perhaps rather better-off, with an estate valued at over £118. Her house was correspondingly more grand, with a parlour, a parlour chamber, a room over the parlour, a buttery chamber, a chamber at the head of the stairs, a room over the house, a lower chamber, an old parlour, a kitchen and a buttery. Despite this apparently quite large house she also seemed to find it necessary to put a bed and its furnishings in the passage, presumably the hall or a landing.

Most of the inventories give an impression that the houses were sparsely furnished, with few comforts. A table, a few chairs and some stools are mentioned in almost all the inventories; some cushions often comprised the bulk of the furnishings. Storage was generally provided by a chest or two, sometimes shelves or a press. Most houses contained a number of beds, and perhaps one or more feather beds and bolsters. Warmth was provided by a few blankets or occasionally a coverlet.

In the kitchen were to be found brass pots and pans, earthenware, wooden vessels, mugs and, almost everywhere, pewter. A number of sieves and riddles are mentioned, which were probably used for preparing grain and meal. One inventory mentions specifically a 'coale cart', which would indicate the use of coal as a fuel at this time, and another lists half a bushell of fuel. Keeping warm would have been quite a problem at that time. Edward Rigby's inventory of 1641 lists rendered tallow valued at four shillings and presumably used for making candles.

At least two inventories list spinning wheels and Richard Barton (1615) had two. They were, however, only worth a shilling each. Further evidence of spinning at home is given in Edward Rigby's inventory, which included yarn worth thirteen shillings.

Among the few luxuries were occasionally to be found items such as a warming pan, looking glasses, glass bottles and glasses, and brass candlesticks. Arthur Finch, who was fairly prosperous when he died in 1636, with an estate valued at over £163, also had one or two more luxuries, with a clock, a desk, and interestingly 'a mapp of the county of Lancaster', possibly a copy of John Speed's map published earlier in the century.

Personal clothing was generally only valued at a pound or two and not itemised, being usually described as 'his apparell'. One exception was the estate of John Rigbie, a poor labourer, who died in 1618. His estate was worth less than £2 and was made up almost entirely of his clothes, which comprised two doubloons, a pair of breeches, one other doubloon and a pair of old breeches, a pair of stockings, a pair of gloves, one pair of shoes, one shirt and a pair of shoes, together with one or two other items. However, the value of the clothing of most other estates was little different to Rigbie's, so one is left with the conclusion that clothing may have been a relatively minor item among many people's possessions.

William Lathom died in 1693, and his estate valued at £95 0*s*. 8*d*.

included, £86 13*s.* in money. The residue included wheat on the ground, value £3, a cow and hay, worth together £2 10*s.*, so that his total other effects were only valued at about £3. They included a feather bed and bolster (£1 5*s.*), two blankets (six shillings), linen (six shillings), some mugs, some pewter, brass, a frying pan and two chests. There is no mention of table or chairs. His estate was divided into three. One third was left to his wife, one third left to his daughter, Alice Aspinwall, who had married a blacksmith from Shevington, and the remaining third went also to his wife after ten shillings had been paid to his nephew, Thomas Lathom.

Jane Lathom made her will in May 1694. She left one shilling each to her daughters Ellen Fisher and Elizabeth Sumner, and one shilling to William, Edward, Thomas and Jane, the children of Alice and Edward Asmall of Shevington, presumably to be divided between them, but the residue of the estate was also to be divided between the four children. Edward Aspinall was to be one of the executors. It is interesting to see three variants of the spelling of his name, two of them in the same document.

These inventories only shed light on a limited aspect of everyday life in seventeenth-century Parbold, but they do give an indication of the relative simplicity of domestic life sweetened with but few luxuries.

Parbold Inventories, 1600–1700

Year	*Name*	*Occupation*	*Value*		
			£	*s.*	*d.*
1615	Richard Barton	yeoman	86	2	6
1618	Jane Lathom	widow			
1618	John Rigby	labourer			
1618	Hugh Mawdesley	tailor			
1636	Arthur Finch	yeoman	163	4	6
1641	Edward Rigby	yeoman	131	5	0
1664	Thomas Patrick		48	16	4
1667	Katherine Wrennell	widow	141	13	8
1665	Richard Barton		73	4	10

Year	*Name*	*Occupation*	*Value*		
1670	John Barton		29	7	0
1672	Richard Lancaster		27	16	8
1675	Edward Rigby		135	9	2
1675	James Bannister		52	12	6
1692	Thomas Lathom	shoemaker	128	14	10
1694	William Lathom	yeoman	95	5	8
1700	Elizabeth Barton	widow	118	1	6

EDUCATION

In 1692 Richard Durning made provision in his will[79] for the founding of a free grammar school in Bispham. His will left his lands in Walton-le-Dale, Wrightington and Parbold so that the income from them should be used for charitable purposes, including annual payments to the highways of Bispham and poor householders in Bispham, an allowance for the binding of a poor child as an apprentice, money to be distributed to the poor relatives of Richard Durning, and £2 to be paid yearly to the minister at Douglas Chapel. After these payments had been made, the balance was to provide the wages for the school master in the school which was set up under the terms of the will.

The original minute and account book of the school is still extant.[80] The original trustees of the charity were Thomas Ashurst, Nicholas Rigbye, Thomas Willson, William Banaster, Henry Carter, Jonathan Wrennal, John Willson, James Schofield and Thomas Whaley. The first school master was Thomas Hall, and it seems likely that the school first started in Parbold on a temporary basis until the new building in Bispham was ready. Thomas Whaley was not only a trustee, but occupied the house, known at that time as Parbold House, which contributed the biggest rent to the trust's income. This house possibly became Common House, since, in accounts for Durning's charity in later years, Parbold House is not mentioned and the highest rent is paid by the occupants of Common House. However, the initials on the datestone of the present Common House, coincidentally dated 1692, would argue

A true Inventorie of all the goods and chattells which weare belonginge unto Arthure ffynch late of Wrightinton in the countie of Lancaster deceased at the tyme of his death praysed the xxth day of ffebruarie Anno dni 1618. by William Holland, Richarde Willson Nicholas Heskine and Nicholas Standishe as followeth, vidzt

Inprimis in the upper Chamber twoo fether bedde twoo boulsters and one pillowe weight vij stones — xlijs
Item three coverlette — xxs
Item three blankete — vs
Item Lynnen — viijs viijd
Item in honnye — vs
Item a cheese crate — iiijd
Item one chiste — vjs
Item one paire of bedstocke — ijs vjd
Item earthen potte and mugge — xijd
Item one silke hatte — xijd
Item a seale and saffegard — iiijs vjd
In the parlor.
Item three coverlette — iiijs
Item one boulster and ij pillowes — vjs
Item an ould blanckett — xijd
Item twoo better coverlette — viijs iiijd
Item iiij blankete and one undercloth — viijs
Item one fether bedd, j boulster and twoo pillowes weight fowr stone — xxviijs
Item a paire of bedstocke — vs

Part of the inventory of Arthur Finch, Yeoman, of Parbold, 1636. (LRO WCW 1636)

against this conclusion. Thomas Whaley lived in Parbold House until about 1710. Whaleys resided in Parbold for many years, and in later times were living in the stone house which is next to the garage at the bottom of the Common. It may, therefore, be that this is the original Parbold House or that the Whaleys moved there later. Durning's school was to be free to all who came, and being only about a mile outside Parbold, almost certainly provided the earliest educational opportunity for the children of Parbold. Some twenty-five years later a school was founded in Newburgh, again within reasonable walking distance of Parbold. Thus, although there was no proper school within Parbold itself, for the times, the village was well served with schooling nearby.

By about 1802, there was a Catholic school at Parbold Hall, but this was short-lived and had removed to Ampleforth by about 1804. In 1806 Parbold Hall was leased by Edward Dicconson to the Rev. John Wadsworth.[81] By 1808 Dr. Wadsworth was running a school at the hall, although it seems unlikely that it was attended by any local children. A letter [82] home to his parents by one of the pupils, Abel Bayley, who came from Staly bridge near Manchester, was written in beautiful copperplate handwriting, and gives details of the arrangements for the Christmas holidays that year.

> Our Christmas holidays will commence on Thursday 22nd instant and we return to school on Monday, the 23rd of January. Mr Wadsworth purposes attending the young gentlemen to Manchester on the day of breaking up and meeting them at Mr Jepson's on their return to school. On account of the shortness of the days we are to set off from Manchester exactly at ten o'clock. I am learning reading, writing, geography, accompts and dancing. I hope the progress I have made in my learning will meet with your approbation. Mr and Mrs Wadsworth present their most respectful compliments to you. Please to give my love to my brothers and sister.
>
> I am dear father and mother
> Your ever dutiful son
> Abel Bayley

The stilted style may reflect the formal relationship between well-off parents and their children of the period, or may indicate, as seems more likely, that the letter was not Abel's own composition, but was more an exercise in copy writing. Certainly a letter from the same boy to his parents at Christmas three years later [83] is written in the same formal manner and with many similar phrases. It also suggests that in 1811 Abel had neither seen nor written to his parents for a long time, since he states 'during the last half year I have enjoyed a good state of health'.

The cost of educating a boy in this manner was about £50 a year including board, education, washing and a myriad of other items, both educational and domestic, as indicated in the account submitted for Abel's education for the half year to June 1812. The miscellaneous items included:

seat in church	4 pence
barber	1 shilling
dancing	2 shillings
military exercise	3 shillings and 6 pence
copy books, pens, ink, paper, fire etc.	1 pound 1 shilling

But all this must have been very remote from the everyday life of the people of Parbold.

The census of 1851 records two women who gave their occupation as school mistress, but where and what form of education they offered is not known. The term 'scholar' as used on census returns is sometimes considered to have little meaning, but an analysis of the 1851 census for Parbold suggests that it was used in a legitimate way. The term is only applied to boys between three and fourteen, and girls between four and fifteen. Moreover, it is only applied to 50 per cent of the boys and 61 per cent of the girls in these age groups. This does not suggest irregular use, at least on the enumerator's part.

The Education Act of 1870 extended and regularised the provision of elementary education, but much of the work was still undertaken by the churches. Parbold National School, run by the Church of England, was built on Parbold Hill using stone from the recently demolished Douglas Chapel. The log books from the school are held by the school and survive from 1878. The education committee for that year was a large one, with ten members. Among the names represented were the familiar Parbold surnames, Rigby and Barton, as well as some other names that were coming to prominence, such as Hugh Ainscough and William Liptrot. In 1880 when the school

Parbold School.
Located on Parbold Hill next to the church, consecrated in 1875, Parbold School was built from stone taken from the demolition of Douglas Chapel. The school was replaced by the present school in the early 1970s.

was inspected,[84] its grant was paid on an average attendance of 33 pupils. There were 14 juniors and 21 other pupils presented for examination. The school was deemed to have done fairly well for a first examination, but the mistress was urged to endeavour to improve the spelling of the lower classes and also improve the arithmetic. Discipline was said—on the whole—to be good. At this time school attendance was still voluntary, compulsory education up to the age of ten not being introduced until the Education Act of 1880.

RECREATION

There is only limited information about how the inhabitants of Parbold spent their leisure time. Life was hard, hours of work were long and the relative level of poverty probably left little time or money for non-essential purposes.

The public houses were probably the main source of entertainment for the ordinary man. There are no particularly early records of inns or public houses in the area, but the *Eagle and Child*, Newburgh (now Derby House Saddlery) occurs in mid-eighteenth-century records, and the *Windmill* and *Chapel House Inn* in Parbold are frequently referred to throughout the nineteenth century.

Shooting was popular for the better-off by the mid-nineteenth century. In 1843 a Mr Case had the shooting rights to Parbold Rabbit Warren, but gave it up in 1845 when it was taken over by a Mr Wagstaff at a rental of £50 *per annum*.[85] Parbold Rabbit Warren is shown on the 1846 Ordnance Survey map on the south side of Parbold Hill, below the Reform Act Monument ('Parbold Bottle'). Although rabbits were raised in warrens for food and their skins as a form of farming,[86] Parbold Rabbit Warren seems to have been used, at least in the mid-nineteenth century, solely for sport. In 1850 the shooting rights were taken over by William Copeland of Liverpool. By 1853 Thomas Morris of Fairhurst Hall agreed to take over the shooting for five years at a rent of £20 *per annum* for the first two years and £40 per year thereafter. Presumably the reduction in rent was due to the interference of the railway which was being constructed at that time. He agreed to leave as good as or a better stock of rabbits for breeding when he was to quit in 1858 as when he took over, but wanted the sole shooting rights on the area between Alder Lane and Appley Lane and between Parbold Hall, Dangerous Corner and the Douglas River. There were some problems with walls and gates on the warren to keep the rabbits in. It is interesting to compare the rental of £50 *per annum* with the wages of the gamekeeper who received £7 10*s*. per quarter (£30 *per annum*).

By 1886 there is an indication of more general time for organised recreation when Parbold Cricket Club agreed a lease for seven years at £1 *per annum*, payable to Mr James Whaley for an approximately six-acre field. The lease was signed on behalf of the cricket club by the Rev. H. P. Owen Smith, J. Teasdale Walker (of Parbold Hall), John Kellet and George Gilroy. The field in question is number 203 on the tithe survey, which is in the vicinity of the present-day Community Centre.

3

Local affairs

EARLY RELIGIOUS LIFE

PARBOLD, at the extreme edge of the parish of Eccleston, was some six miles or so distant from the parish church. However, from early days the religious needs of the people of Parbold and the surrounding area were served by Douglas Chapel, a small chapel dedicated to St Mary, and located in a remote spot close to the river and adjacent to the present-day Chapel House Farm at the bottom of Chapel Lane. Just when the chapel was established is uncertain. It has been claimed [87] that an old tradition states that it was built to commemorate a victory of the Saxons over the Danes, but there is no evidence to substantiate this. It has also been said [88] that it was probably founded by the Knights of St John, who held lands nearby for the use of their tenants, but again the evidence is uncertain.

The chapel's history seems to be traceable back to at least 1240, when a reference was made to 'John, Priest of Douglas'.[89] Further mention is found in 1292, when William was the chaplain. The chapel was in use until 1875, when it was finally pulled down, and a detailed account of the building and photographs survive. The building was considered to date back to about 1420, but it had been restored and enlarged at various times. Even so, at the end of its life it was still considered to be a curious and simple place with no brasses or monuments, and with six roughly hewn wooden columns, thick with paint and supported on stone pedestals, which supported the roof.

The chapel was not richly endowed; when King Henry VIII's commissioners arrived following the Reformation, they found only a single eight-ounce chalice and one vestment. By 1610 the chapel was in disuse, there being no minister, but in 1619, John Bridgeman, who had formerly been Rector of Wigan, became Bishop of Chester

Chapel House Inn. Photographed in 1975, when the words 'Southport Brewery Co.' could be made out on the side of the building.

The site of Douglas Chapel, shown by a stone cross, and nearby Chapel House Farm.

A view of Douglas Chapel.

and set about renovating the churches in his diocese. Douglas Chapel benefited by having glass put into the windows, including one stained-glass window. Further improvements took place in 1648, when a new pulpit was installed; this was subsequently moved to Christ Church, Parbold, in 1875.

The Lathom family are considered to have had connections with Douglas Chapel from early days. During a dispute of 1526, William Lathom and his ancestors were said to have been founders and patrons of the chapel 'without tyme of mynde'. The family retained the advowson of Eccleston (that is the right to appoint the rector) until 1730.

Douglas Chapel will reappear in our story from time to time, but it seems certain that it was an ancient foundation and played a more important role in the day-to-day religious activities of the village than the remote and distant mother church.

THE CIVIL WARS

The considerable activity taking place within just a few miles of Parbold during the civil wars between King Charles I and Parliament, between 1642 and 1651, cannot but have impinged upon the daily lives of the people of the district, but it would be interesting to find details of this involvement.

Lathom House was besieged twice, in 1644 and 1645, by parliamentarians who travelled from Wigan via Standish to Lathom, and therefore must have passed through Parbold. It is claimed that they damaged Douglas Chapel, which they used for stabling their horses,[90] and also that there was a skirmish between the two sides near Gilliburne's House, which has been identified as Gillibrands.[91]

The Lancashire gentry who supported the king came largely from the west and north of the county, whilst those with parliamentarian sympathies were concentrated in the south and east, in an area centred on Manchester and Bolton. The main families around

Another view of Douglas Chapel.

The interior of Douglas Chapel, showing the box pews and two of the six rough-hewn timber pillars supporting the roof.

Parbold were generally royalists, although there were several notable exceptions, including Peter Caterall of Crook, Robert Mawdesley of Mawdesley and Thomas Wilson of Tunley, Wrightington, who all ultimately declared their allegiance to Parliament.[92] Richard

Lathom, lord of the manor of Parbold, a young man of twenty when war started in 1643, supported the King and took part in the attack on Lancaster in that year, during which the town was set on fire.

The sympathies of the ordinary village folk are not known. It would be interesting to know whether Richard Lathom recruited any of the local people before he went off to fight, or whether there were local conscripts or volunteers among the defenders or besiegers of Lathom House. Undoubtedly, the events taking place locally must have caused quite a stir, and the village did not escape totally unscathed. Evidence is provided by the petition of Hugh Rigbie of Parbold, who petitioned the justices of the peace at Wigan in January 1649,[93] that he should be excused from being constable of the township, because although it was the custom for the post to go to householders, he was not one since his cottage had been 'accidentallie burned to the ground by Colonell Shutleworth's soldiers'.

The aftermath of the civil war was considerable. Richard Lathom was tried for treason in 1652, and his estates sequestrated.[94] Following sequestration a committee was set up with the objective of obtaining, firstly, a confession from the offender, then a pledge of adherence to the government, and finally, a full account of the offenders possessions. The offender was then allowed to compound a fine according to the level of guilt, being one sixth of his estate if he took part on the king's side in either of the civil wars, or one third if he was active in both wars.[95]

Parbold was surveyed in 1653. Amongst the estate is mentioned a dwelling-house called Parbold Hall and a watermill, 400 timber trees and several lands and tenements occupied by various persons and valued at £84 4*s.* 10*d.* *per annum*. The manor house was let by the sequestrators for seven years at a rental of £95 12*s.* 6*d.* in 1651. Although the Lathom family had recovered their lands before 1660 through the purchase on their behalf by trustees (George Hurd, a London agent acquired Parbold for £3,331, and John Sumner of Midhurst, Sussex, bought Allerton for £2,749 12*s.* 2*d.*), the family failed to regain their previous position.[96] At the outbreak of the civil war the family were financially sound; afterwards, they were not so. Allerton was sold off in 1670 and Parbold mortgaged to John Crisp, a London money lender. Crisp eventually foreclosed in 1680, and thereby became lord of the manor. Although the Lathoms continued to live in the district, they lived in mediocre obscurity.

LAW AND ORDER

An important aspect in the administration of any community, even a small rural one, is the manner in which disputes are settled. Although there do not appear to be any surviving records of local manorial courts which regulated the affairs on behalf of the lord of the manor, it seems certain that they existed in Parbold, since in appraising Richard Lathom's estate, which was confiscated at the end of the civil wars, the commissioners stated that 'Richard Lathom was seised of . . . court baron and court leet fines two shillings and sixpence.'

More significant are the quarter sessions, the origins of which date back to the mid-fourteenth century, although the term was not used until late in the following century. The power of these courts varied somewhat over the years, but they were basically set up to act as keepers of the peace and justices of oyer and terminer. That is to say, they could deal with a range of matters ranging from the administration of the poor law through to serious criminal matters. As the name implies, the courts met quarterly, at Easter, Midsummer, Michaelmas and Epiphany. The Lancashire quarter sessions met at a number of places, but Parbold business was almost exclusively carried out at the sessions held at Ormskirk at Easter and Midsummer and at Wigan at Michaelmas and Epiphany. The justices were local residents, often with intimate knowledge of local affairs and conditions and were appointed from the local gentry. They were required to be resident within the county and had to possess land of a minimum value of £20 *per annum*. Many of the potential Lancashire justices were unable to serve because of their refusal to conform to the new religion following the Reformation, which probably accounts for the absence of any Parbold names listed amongst the Lancashire justices for the period 1603 to 1642.[97] Lancashire quarter sessions records survive from the end of the sixteenth century, and are held in the Lancashire Record Office.

The justices were appointed to serve at county level. For the hundreds (Parbold was in Leyland Hundred), high constables were appointed, whilst at a more local level, the important parish or township officers were the churchwardens and overseers of the poor. Within the township itself, the most important office was that of constable. The surveyor of highways was the other local township official.

THE TOWNSHIP CONSTABLE

The constable was the chief keeper of the peace and upholder of the law within the township. He was usually required to attend the quarter sessions when they were held locally. The post, which was unpaid, was appointed by the justices at the quarter sessions, and although important, was, in general, not popular with the villagers whose turn it was to be appointed. Consequently, there are many instances on record of people trying to avoid it. The usual practice was for the post to proceed in strict rotation from house to house. We have already seen how Hugh Rigbie sought to avoid the post on the basis that his house had been destroyed, and that the appointment was on the basis of dwellings and not on the mere holding of land.

There is also evidence [100] that in Parbold an unusual practice had been observed, when it was decided that Edward Gillibrand should serve as constable when the turn of his tenants came round 'according to the custom of the township.' No doubt his tenants were much relieved, although how Edward Gillibrand felt about it is not recorded.

The duties of the constable were wide ranging, and not likely to lead to popularity amongst one's fellow villagers. They included collecting taxes and local rates, maintaining local means of punishment such as the stocks, inspecting ale houses and suppressing gaming houses, to keep a look out for rogues and vagabonds and organising the removal from the township of itinerant beggars and vagrants, apprenticing pauper children, taking charge of lunatics and taking proceedings against local offenders. The appointment was for one year, and although technically appointed by the justices, as we shall see, seems to have been upon the nomination of the township.

Summary justice was dispensed by placing offenders in the stocks, which was usually sited in a prominent position, frequently near the church. Douglas Chapel was not in a prominent position, and the stocks in Parbold was set up near the present *Stocks Tavern.* Bulpit [98] relates that Parbold stocks came to a sudden end when a drunkard was released by a friend one Sunday morning with a saw and hatchet, the pair then proceeding to destroy the stocks. He does not, however, record when this is supposed to have happened.

Further attempts to avoid the post of constable are those of Thomas Orrell in 1657 [99] and Richard Lancaster in 1656.[100] Thomas Orrell complained that he only possessed a small cottage with a little garden containing scarcely three roods of ground (about three-quarters of an acre), and that the other inhabitants of Parbold were seeking to impose the duty of constable upon him, which he considered to be unfair and contrary to the law. Furthermore, he complained that the task was more than he was able to perform. Richard Lancaster petitioned the magistrates at Wigan on 19 January 1656 to be excused the post of constable because he had already served as constable two years previously on account of a small messuage (house) with two acres which he held, but that he was now being nominated to serve for a further term because on another part of the land there had previously stood a small cottage some twenty years or so before. The magistrates ruled that the township should nominate another, more suitable candidate.

Surprisingly, it appears that the post of constable was occasionally filled by women equally as men, Mary Lathom having been constable of Parbold in 1699.[101] The following year she was exempted from serving following a petition being raised to seek her exemption, which was signed both by the trustees of the newly erected Bispham School, who also held lands in Parbold, and also by a number of Parbold residents. The main reason cited was that the land for which she could be liable had no dwelling upon it, and the land was, in any case, under rack rent to Mr Crisp of Parbold Hall.

The unpopularity of the post is further illustrated by the petition of Robert Simson in 1657.[102] Simson, a younger son, had already served over a year as constable on behalf of his elderly father, aged about 88, and his equally elderly mother who had been called upon to serve as constable. Because they were both poor, they were unable to pay anyone else to serve in their places, so that Simson

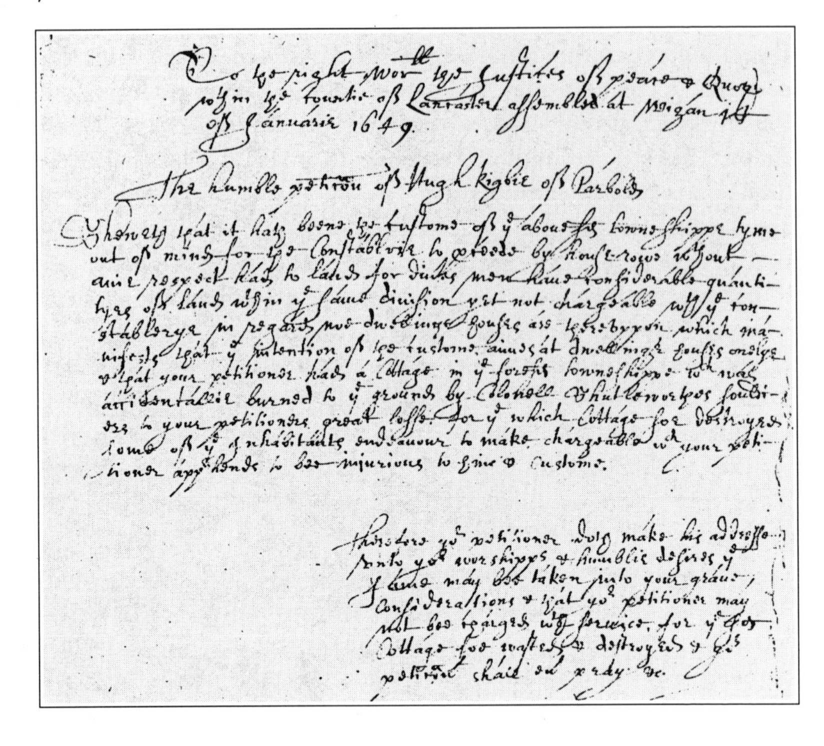

To the right worll the Justices of peace & Quorum within the countie of Lancaster assembled at Wigan 14th of Januarie 1649.

The humble petition of Hugh Rigbie of Parbold

Sheweth that it hath beene the custome of ye above sd towneshippe tyme out of minde for the Constablerie to procede by house rowe without anie respect had to landes for dutys now have considerable quantityes of landes within ye same division yet not chargeable with ye constablerye in regard noe dwellinge houses are thereuppon which manifestly that ye intention of the custome aimes at dwellinge houses onlye. That your petitioner had a Cottage in ye foresaid towneshippe wch was accidentallie burned to ye ground by Colonell Whittleworthes souldiers to your petitioners great losse. For ye which Cottage soe destroyed some of ye inhabitants endeavour to make chargeable wth your petitioner [illegible] to bee injurious to time & Custome.

Therefore yor petitioner doth make his addresse unto yor worshipps & humble desires ye same may bee taken into your grave considerations & that yor petitioner may not bee charged with service for ye sd Cottage soe wasted & destroyed & yor petitioner shall ever pray &c.

The petition of Hugh Rigbie, seeking to be excused the constable's duties, 1649–50. (LRO QSP 27/24)

had given up his work to stand in their stead. Although the term of office had ended in January, a new constable had not been appointed because of arguments within the township, so that Simson had now served nearly an extra four months. He requested that an order should be made whereby the township should pay him for the time that had passed since his year had been up. His petition was granted. This petition is also interesting, since it shows that if you could afford it, then you could buy exemption.

The constable was required regularly to give to the justices an account of misdemeanours in the township. Parbold was probably a relatively peaceful area. Edward Lancaster, for example, when required as constable to make presentments at the quarter sessions in July 1665, reported that there had not been any misdemeanours.[103] However, the following year, a warrant was issued by the high constable for the apprehension of Thomas Cornwell, Hugh Hawett,

John Hawett, Ralph Woodcock, William Barron and James Matthew for having committed several misdemeanours against their neighbours, including forcibly entering land and cutting trees and disturbing the peace. This document [104] is worth quoting in full:

> Com Lanc fforasmuch as credible informacon is given unto us, two of his ma[jes]ties justices of peace and quor[um] within the said county that sev[er]all p[er]sons within yo[u]r towneshippe vidzt Thomas Cornwell, Hugh Hawett John Hawett Raph Woodcock Henry Woodcock William Baron and James Walthew, are all of them men of evill behaviour, And have comitted sev[er]all misdemanors against their neighbours and besides many other things which are objected against them they have forcibly antred in to their neighbours grounds and cutt and spoyled their timber, to the great disturbance of his ma[jes]ties peace and abuse to his people Therefore on the behalfe of our sov[er]aigne Lord the King wee strictly charg and comand you and every of you that you omitt not but doe forthw[i]th upon receipt hereof app[re]hend and take the bodyes of the said Thos Cornwell, Hugh Hawett, John Hawett Raph Woodcock Henry Woodcock William Baron and James Matthew, and bring them before us, or the one of us, to finde sufficent suerties as well [above line] for their good abeareing towards our sov[er]aigne Lord the King and all his leige people untill the next gen[er]all Quarter Sessions of the peace to bee holden for the hundred of Leyland in the County afore said and alsoe for their p[er]sonall appearances then & there to answer such matters as shall be laid to their charge, And if they or any of them shall refuse soe to doe that then you him or them convey or cause to be conveyd to his ma[jest]ies Gaole at Lancaster there to remayne untill hee or they shall willingly doe the same, And soe that you certifie yo[u]r doeings in the p[re]misses to the said justices at the said sessions bringing thither this p[re]cept w[i]th you And hereof faile not at your p[er]ills Given und[er] our hands and seales the sixteenth day of August A[nn]o R.Rs Caroli s[e]c[un]di Angl[orum] et[c] decimo octavo Aoq^{u} dni (A[nn]oqu[e] d[omi]ni) 1666
>
> To all Sheriffes Maiors Bayliffes Constables subconstables and all other his Ma[jes]ties officers w[i]thin the said County, And especially to ye constables of Wrightington and Parbold
>
> These
>
> Truly Executed & bound over to the sessions by mr. Entwhisle
>
> Henry Slater
>
> Will: Farrington

The warrant for the apprehension of Thomas Cornwell, Hugh Hawett, and others, 1666. (Transcribed in full in the text.) (LRO QSP 296/7)

THE VESTRY

The parish exercised a considerable influence over the organisation and administration of local affairs through its principal officers, the churchwardens and overseers of the poor. The churchwardens were important local officers, and had several duties, including the keeping down of vermin and pests, the maintenance of the fabric of the church and its property as well as keeping the parish accounts. These accounts were presented to the parishioners at an annual parish vestry meeting. Vermin and pests included hedgehogs, sparrows, jays, magpies and foxes. Generally, a bounty was paid upon the presentation of the heads of the offending creatures.

The distance of Parbold from the mother church at Eccleston, and the problems which this could present, is recognised in the report of the Lancashire Church Survey of 1650.[105] It was recognised that it was:

> . . . fitt and necessarie that the towne of Parbold and the south and south west side of Wrightington abutting towards Parbold and lying nearer unto Dugles than any other church and chappell be appropriated and united there unto . . .

and that the tythes from the district should go towards the support of a preaching minister there. At the time of the survey, William Broadsword was minister and had for his stipend the interest on two small gifts and £50 per year from the Rector of Eccleston. This report recognises a degree of autonomy for Douglas Chapel, and this is further evidenced in the surviving churchwardens' accounts for Eccleston parish, which are extant from 1712 onwards.[106]

The parish meeting was held annually at Easter to consider the churchwardens' primary accounts, to elect the churchwardens, sidesmen and overseers of the poor for the coming year, and to raise a parish rate. A second meeting was held in the summer to consider the colateral and final accounts. The parish was considered in two parts, and officers were elected to serve separately for Eccleston-with-Heskin and Parbold-with-Wrightington, churchwardens' accounts being presented in a similar manner.

The account books provide interesting and detailed accounts of expenses, as well as parish activities and a complete list of officers for the townships for the period 1712 to 1825. Many names familiar to Parbold history appear, including Gillibrand, Tunstall, Barton, Hawett and Lancaster.

The accounts for one year give an idea of the range of expenses. The example below is from 1740.

The Primary Accts of John Willson, Church Warden for Wrightington & Parbold, for the Year 1740

Spent at settling the former Church Wardens accounts		9	0
Court Fees		2	0
Spent at the Court		4	0
For Seven Gallons & a half of Wine	2	5	0
For carriage at three Several times		1	6
Mrs Doro. Hodgson for surplice	2	5	0
To the Ringers for their Sallary	3	0	0
For a lock for the Church Gate			5
For Lether for the Bells and fettling them		1	2
For a Coard for the font			1½
To a Glazier		1	0
Spent oth' Glazier			4
For a Proclamation Book and Almanack			6
Postage for the New Prayers			4
The Blacksmiths Bill		1	8
The Carpenters Bill		5	4
The Clark for four journeys to Douglas Chappel		1	3
Spent at Drawing Presentments		1	0
Seth Rigbys Bill		7	9
Rich. Hatchs Bill		5	0
Spent at the rejoycing day for Adm[iral] Vernon		1	6
Spent on Strange Preachers		4	11½
Spent when the new Rector came		2	5
Spent upon the Parisioners who came to visit		3	½
For Bottles and Corks		2	0

For a Fox head			6
For Ley Books		1	0
For an Almanack for the Chappel			2
Spent at Settling these accounts		1	2
Robt. Pemberton his Sallary		5	0
For mending the Chappel Windows &c		1	3½
The Clark of Douglas Chappel his Sallary		10	0
Mr Hodgson for Drawing a Presentment			6
	12	15	5

These accounts were passed at the Easter meeting held on 30 March. A subsequent meeting was held in the summer to consider the colateral accounts, which were presented as follows:

Spent at Easter Meeting		14	7½
Spent when Chorley singers came to Eccleston		1	3
Spent at Douglas Chappel when some singars came		1	3
Court Fees		2	6
Spent at the Court		5	0
For cleaning the Church windows, Steeple, Flaggs &c		4	2½
James Bate for Whipping Dogs		4	3
For Parchment doing the Register		1	0
Spent at Drawing Presentments		1	6
For New Bell Roaps		2	6
For washing the Linen at Douglas Chappel		3	6
For Copying the Register		2	0
For Drawing & Entring both former and Collateral accts		2	6
For Elizabeth Weldon for a Wiscat, Beesoms, Coard, & Candles			6¼
	2	12	1¼
Primary accounts	12	15	5
	15	7	6¼

Items clearly varied from year to year, but the above accounts seem to be fairly typical. The price paid for foxheads seemed to vary considerably from between six pence and three shillings.

The largest item, surprisingly, is the ringer's salary. Bell ringing seems to have been a profitable activity. So much so that at the parish meeting of 1736 a resolution had been passed that:

> agreed . . . for the future no more Money or expences be allow'd the Ringers, and charged upon the parish, than the summe of two shillings amongst them all for ale, for each rejoycing & ringing day. Also agreed . . . that all Parishoners for the future, who shall attend any general & publick or other parish meeting to be warn'd call'd or held, that every person shall attend at his own Expence and charge and that the parish be freed from the same in all accounts hereafter to be brought in.

An attached list of agreed ringing days gives an interesting record of the important public days recognised at that time. These were as follows:

20 January	Prince of Wales born
15 April	Duke William born
29 May	Restoration of King Charles II
11 June	King's Accession
11 October	King's Coronation
30 October	King's Birthday
5 November	Gunpowder Plot
25 December	Christmas Day

In the mid-nineteenth century there is growing evidence of the separation of Parbold from Eccleston in practical terms and before the legal establishment of Parbold as a civil parish, with the holding of a vestry meeting within Parbold itself. Minutes of the vestry meetings survive from 1852.[107] The meetings were held at Chapel House and usually close to Easter. The main business was the drawing up of lists of fit and proper people to serve as the principal officers of the township, in particular overseer of the poor, surveyor of the highways and assessor of the Queen's taxes. At the 1852 meeting, Richard Swift was appointed as surveyor of the highways at four guineas for the year. John Conder was to be paid £1 10*s*. for catching moles. Appointing a rat catcher appears to have been less straightforward: John Greer and Hugh Ainscough were appointed to engage a person to kill rats. Vermin must have been a considerable problem, since in 1855 John Holland was appointed to kill rats for a sum not exceeding £12 per year, for which he was to attend four times a year at £3 a time. Mole catching was probably a skilled art. At least they were not necessarily local people: Thomas Huck from near Kendal was appointed mole catcher in 1874.

In 1879 it was resolved to hold future meetings at *Mill House Inn*, since holding meetings at Chapel House Inn was rather inconvenient. At the same meeting it was agreed that the box containing the parish records should be moved there, and an inventory of documents was to be made. Unfortunately, this does not seem to have survived. As the century progressed more and more of the bureaucratic trappings of modern local administrative activities came within the remit of the local vestry meeting with the setting-up of a local Education Committee, a local School Attendance Committee and a local Sanitary Committee.

THE CHURCH

In Parbold there remained strong adherence among many for the old Roman Catholic faith. West Derby and Leyland Hundreds were among the two districts in Lancashire in which Roman Catholics were most numerous,[108] and within the Leyland Hundred, Wrightington and Parbold had, with 64, the second highest number of convicted Catholic recusants in 1638, being exceeded only by Chorley, with 72. This represents a very significant percentage of the adult population.

The recusant roll for 1628 [109] gives the names of all convicted 'popish recusants' aged seventeen or above, and all non-communicants aged twenty-one or above, who were to pay a fine of 8*d*. The actual amounts collected in Wrightington and Parbold for 64 offenders were exactly twice this amount (total £4 5*s*. 4*d*.) presumably indicating that all those were convicted on both counts. Names include Nelson (of Fairhurst Hall), Rigby, Hawett, Fisher, Bimson, Barton, Lancaster and Lathom, all of which, except Nelson, are common Parbold family names.

The continuation of Catholicism is again seen in 1679 and 1680 when petitions were presented at the quarter sessions to have the fines of poor Catholic recusants waived.[110, 111]

In 1804, further information about Catholicism in the district is contained in a report to the Bishop of Chester which cited that there are 67 papists and one person perverted by marrying a papist woman, within the Chapelry of Douglas. There were three places where Catholics assembled, namely Wrightington Hall, Parbold Hall and Fairhurst Hall. At that time the priest at Parbold was Richard Marsh, who also ran a boys' Catholic school at the hall, which subsequently moved to Ampleforth and became the public school of that name.

Parbold Hall seems to have had fluctuating fortunes in its associations with nonconformity: in 1709 Isabella Crisp had petitioned that the manor house called Parbold Hall should be recorded as a meeting place for dissenting Protestants.[112]

After about 1804 the main Catholic meeting place for the area became Wrightington Hall, until the formal opening of the Church of Our Lady and All Saints, Parbold, in 1884. The proposal to build a Catholic church in Parbold stemmed from a desire by Hugh and Richard Ainscough of the milling family to endow a church in Parbold, to be served by the Benedictines. This project passed from conception to consecration in the short space of eight years,[113] and marked the continuation of the tradition of Catholicism in the township dating back to Richard Lathom, 'the Great Papist', who lost the manor of Parbold through supporting the wrong side against Parliament.

In the meantime, as we have seen, Douglas Chapel had in practice been slowly becoming more and more independent of the mother church at Eccleston. The chapel acted as a centre of worship for a wide area. Its influence in this respect can still be seen in the way that a number of footpaths converged on the chapel, and a footbridge, serving the needs of the area south of the River Douglas is still maintained nearby. In 1801 [114] it was decided that the chapel was too small to accommodate the population which had increased considerably within three miles of the chapel, and it was decided to build a gallery at the west end, 37 feet wide and 12 feet broad, and with a staircase through the existing porch. The gallery was completed early in 1804. The pews were sold for sums between

£14 and £33, the total sale raising £176 7*s.* 6*d.* The purchasers of the pews were indicative of the geographical spread of the area from which the worshippers came. Only one of a dozen pews was sold to a Parbold resident, the others being bought by churchgoers from Bispham, Lathom, Newburgh and Wrightington. The trustees for this project were John Johnson, the curate at the chapel, James Rigby, Ralph Culshaw, Nathan Tunstall, James Ranicars, William Wright and Thomas Bimson, yet again a fair cross section of well-known local names.

Further evidence of the way in which the chapel served a wider area than Parbold is provided by the records for baptisms at the chapel in the period 1809–12.[115] Only 20% were from Parbold, the largest number (43%) being from Wrightington, but candidates for baptism also came from Lathom, Dalton, Newburgh, Bispham and even Mawdesley, Shevington, Upholland and Ormskirk.

Yet a further step towards independence came in 1862, when the *London Gazette* of 7 January carried a notice of the setting up of a district Chapelry of Douglas,[116] allowing the publication of banns, baptisms, churchings and burials to be solemnised, the fees paid going to the minister for the time being. Over the years a number of relatively small endowments had been made,[117] which no doubt made the life of the incumbent rather less burdensome than before. In 1829, John Price became the curate in charge, and was succeeded by his son William who was to remain in charge until shortly before the consecration of the new church, when he died suddenly. The Prices had charge for 55 years, and it was reported,[118] that 'anxiety to complete the new church at Parbold have undoubtedly hastened the death of the lamented gentleman'.

The new church of Christ Church was built as a result of a desire of Miss Ellen Morris of Fairhurst Hall to replace the old Douglas Chapel and build a new church in memory of her mother. The Morris family had worshipped regularly at the chapel for many years. Consent for the new church was obtained from the Bishop of Manchester, and the Rector of Eccleston, and the site was presented by Sir Thomas Fermor Hesketh of Rufford on long-standing Hesketh lands. The church was consecrated by the Bishop of Manchester on Thursday, 28 October 1875.

LIFE IN THE VICTORIAN VILLAGE

The census return for 1841 is the first to provide anything more than the barest information, and the returns for the period 1841 to 1881 give an interesting picture of life in the Victorian village. During this period the population rose by just over a hundred, or twenty-five per cent. Whilst this represents a faster rate of increase for Parbold than in the previous two hundred years, it is below the national increase, which might perhaps suggest that migration away from the village was beginning to take place.

The township consisted of about ninety households, each averaging just over five persons, including, where appropriate, servants. The centre of the village was based on Mill Lane between the area of the stocks and the Windmill, gradually extending down Station Road after the arrival of the railway. The annual progress of this building activity is clearly evident from the datestones on the houses. However, much of the population was scattered in small pockets or hamlets well away from the centre, some of which have now been either completely abandoned or considerably reduced in size. A hamlet which has now been completely abandoned, leaving little trace on the ground, is that at Newcotts Fold, some three hundred and fifty metres north of Parbold Hall, but which supported a population of some twenty souls living in three households in 1851. Similarly, the cottages which made up the small hamlet close to Gillibrand House have now been destroyed.

There were between ten and fifteen farms, and excluding the Parbold Hall Farm of some two hundred and fifty acres, the average size of holding was quite small, being less than forty acres. Agriculture was the prime employment of about forty-five per cent of the work force in 1841, but this proportion gradually declined to less than twenty per cent by the end of the forty-year period. Coal mining had ceased in the village before 1841, but in 1871 and 1881 there was a small number of people claiming mining as their occupation—presumably either they were retired or travelling to collieries outside the village. Quarrying was active throughout the period, but employing widely varying numbers from year to year. The canal provided work for about five per cent of the work force throughout this period, either as boat builders or boatmen. Similarly, the mill provided a small, but steady source of employment. With the coming of the railway a new and regular source of jobs opened up offering a few jobs, and from 1861 there was a steadily increasing number employed in brickmaking at Parbold brickworks.

In 1841 there were eleven people whose occupation was described as cotton weavers. By 1851 this had reduced to two, and thereafter the occupation is no longer recorded. Other minority occupations included a watchmaker (1841), a shepherd, tanners and shoemakers. The village was probably reasonably self-sufficient with craftsmen such as wheelwrights, saddlers, blacksmiths and nailmakers. The latter two occupations were very much family traditions, the Molyneuxs being the blacksmiths with the Myers making nails.

Although the National School was not set up until after the 1870 Education Act, education was available in Parbold prior to this date, a school mistress and two school masters being recorded as early as the 1841 census.

In 1841 the second biggest employment category could be described as 'in service', occupying over twenty per cent of the population, both male and female. In subsequent years this dropped to about ten per cent, and the increasing range in employment opportunities, and possible growth of the village as a dormitory area with the increased mobility provided by the railway is indicated by the increasing numbers of tradesmen and professional people, including an accountant and a civil engineer, and the increasing difficulty in grouping occupations together. No impression of real poverty is evident. Very few people are ever recorded as of no occupation, and the highest numbers of paupers recorded is four in 1851, two of whom were former weavers.

An interesting occupation is landscape artist, given by John Teasdale Walker, the presumably wealthy occupier of Parbold Hall in 1881. To date records of only three of his paintings have come to light,[119] all of which were of North Wales, and which were sent to the Liverpool autumn exhibitions in 1882 and 1883, and which were offered for sale at between five and seven guineas. It would seem certain that he must have practised his art in the Parbold area, and that local pictures must exist somewhere.

In 1861, over forty per cent of the people living in the village had been born there, whilst nearly eighty per cent had been born within five miles of Parbold village centre, or therefore within convenient walking distance. Only five per cent or twenty-five people had come from more than a hundred miles away, including one Irish family, and the most travelled member of the community, who had been born in Buenos Aires. Three people did not know their place of birth.

From the early nineteenth century onwards, directories become an increasingly useful source of local history information. The situation in Parbold is complicated, since the village is not clearly identified with any of the larger places round about. Early Wigan directories do not list Parbold, although it is included in *Worralls Wigan Directory* of 1869. Baines' *Lancashire Directory* of 1825 includes Parbold. Directories from the later part of the nineteenth century tend to include Parbold with Southport. All these directories give the names and occupations of the principal inhabitants.

4

Work

FARMING

As a rural community, farming will have always been the most important activity in the Parbold area up to the First World War. In the mid-nineteenth century approximately half the working population was engaged in farming on about a dozen farms, and in earlier centuries almost everybody must have been engaged in the production of food to a greater or lesser extent. There is no evidence of open field farming in the district, and there are no enclosure awards. The earliest detailed map (1786) shows a landscape of small enclosed fields, and the old field names, as discussed earlier, would suggest enclosure from a relatively early date. Most of the early field boundaries have since been removed as fields have been enlarged, but a number of remaining field boundaries are dry stone walls, stone probably being the most readily available material at the time the boundaries were established.

The early thirteenth-century deeds of Cockersand Abbey make reference to the right of common pasture and 'acquaintance of pannage' for the demesne pigs of the man dwelling upon the land to which reference is made.

The earliest information concerning farming in the district is probably that collected by Rodgers [120] in his study of land use in Tudor Lancashire. From the evidence available in Final Concords,[121, 122] which are basically conveyances and which give some indication of land use, he was able to produce land use maps. There is a drawback in this method in that the land is not accurately detailed and the actual land listed may be in one or more townships, but nonetheless it gives a broad indication of the picture. Within the district which Rodgers called 'The Parbold Township Group', covering 2,051 acres, he identified 576 acres as 'waste'. Of the remaining 1,475 acres, 55% was under arable use, 11% was meadow, and 34% pasture. The actual area of Parbold is only 1,159 acres, and the remainder of Rodgers' area was in adjacent townships.

The need to improve land in order to get the best out of it has been recognised to a greater or lesser extent since the earliest days of agriculture. In Parbold manure is listed in inventories from the seventeenth century, so its value must have been recognised, and the references to John Legh's injuries received in an accident in a marl pit in 1626 are indicative of marling being practised at least as early as that date. More recently the canal allowed manure, both as animal manure and in the form of 'night soil' from Liverpool, to be brought into the district, and there was also a considerable trade in lime, which was frequently carried as limestone and then burned near to the point of use. A lime kiln in Parbold is referred to in the Poor Rate book of 1833, and a lime kiln is shown on the banks of the Leeds and Liverpool Canal in the tithe award map of 1837. The ruins of this kiln can still be found, but on private land, just to the west of the windmill.

The best source of information on the farms and farmers in the period 1600 to 1750 appears to be that which can be extracted from surviving wills and inventories. Wills of eight Parbold residents described as 'yeoman', and one described as 'husbandman', are available for this period. Others, whose occupation is either not given or is of a non-agricultural occupation, were clearly involved in farming to some extent and add to the picture which can be formed. These inventories generally list the cattle, crops and farm implements first, followed by the household effects, and finally some reference to the deceased's apparel. Generally, the farming effects have by far the highest value.

The earliest inventory which we have is that of Richard Barton, who died in 1615. His estate was valued at between £80 and £90, and over seventy per cent of this was in farming. He appears to have been relatively prosperous, his inventory including:

4 kyne	14		
5 heffers	12	6	8
2 bullocks	5		
4 calves	4	13	4
2 horses and 1 mare	11		

2 swyne	2	
in barley beanes and oats	7	6
in hay	3	

These items show a varied range of livestock and at least four types of crops being cultivated. Among the implements were two ploughs and two harrows, worth only a few shillings, various carts, axletrees and an ox yoke, cattle then being used primarily for ploughing.

Jane Lathom was a widow who died in 1618 and, according to her inventory, was not described as involved in farming. However, her estate was not dissimilar to that of Richard Barton, and just as varied, with four kyne, three calves, one hog, four sheep, four geese and two mares amongst the livestock, and carts, a harrow and a pair of plough irons among the implements. This was the general pattern to a greater or lesser extent. Edward Rigby's inventory (1641) gives some idea of the hand tools used, with spades, hatchets, sickles and rakes. Produce left by Edward Rigby included meal, groates, butter, 'flesh' (presumably meat), grease and cheese. The total value of the produce was £6 2*s.*, a not inconsiderable sum, and must have

Parbold lime kilns, located near the windmill, beside the canal.

represented quite a substantial stock. Crops grown were equally varied, Thomas Patrick (1663) having fifty bushells of oats at the mill and some corn (worth £2 10*s.* 8*d.*), and four bushells of oats and a little barley and malt at home.

The estate of John Barton (1706) showed him to be a relatively prosperous small farmer, with six milking cows, two bullocks, three heifers, four stirks, two horses and a mare, twelve sheep, four pigs and geese and poultry on the five acres he leased. His effects included a wide range of farm equipment, and his spacious house contained such luxuries as a mirror, whiteware and a clock. His house included two parlours, three chambers, a buttery, and what was described as the old kitchen and the old house. This may imply that the house had possibly been rebuilt fairly recently, which would not be too surprising, this being the period from which a major rebuilding of houses stems.

The overall picture is of a varied agriculture, with small numbers of a wide range of beasts being kept and a diverse range of crops being grown. Holdings were small, due mainly to the labour intensive means of cultivation which were all that was available at that time.

Even by the time of the tithe survey in 1837, and the census of 1851, which together give us a detailed picture of farming in the village in the mid-nineteenth century, the typical holding was only a few acres. The 1851 census lists eighteen farmers and gives the size of their holdings. These range from 3 acres to 281 acres (Parbold Hall). Five of the farms were obviously larger than the rest, being those based on Lancaster House (82 acres), Delf House (72 acres), Gillibrand House (76 acres), and Chapel House (75 acres), as well as Parbold Hall. Excluding these farms, the average farm size was a mere seventeen and a half acres. The farms listed in 1851 accounted in total for 813 acres, or about seventy per cent of the total area of the township. The distribution of holdings as it was in 1837 can be clearly seen from the tithe map, and was probably little different by 1851.

The 1851 census lists forty agricultural labourers within the township, and assuming that the farmers occupying the larger holdings were 'gentlemen farmers', then this would indicate 813 acres being worked by 53 workers, or about one worker to fifteen acres. A number of the census entries give the number of workers employed. Parbold Hall Farm employed seventeen workers (16½ acres per worker), Delf House, six workers (12 acres per worker), whilst some of the smaller holdings employed one worker to five or six acres.

Details of the actual land use on the Parbold Demesne Farm, run by Francis Twining for the two years 1869–70, have been recorded [123] together with the details of the individual fields, crops grown and counts on quality and so on. The actual use of the land was as follows:

	1869			*1870*		
	A	R	P	A	R	P
grass	62	2	30	61	1	38
arable wheat	16	0	27	7	00	27
flax	9	2	21	8	1	24
oats	8	1	34	19	2	16
lanes etc		3	30		3	30
	1	2	36	1	2	36
railway	1	1	0	1	1	0
homestead	2	0	13	2	0	13

These figures show quite considerable changes particularly in the relative proportions of wheat and oats grown from year to year.

By the time that Parbold ceased to be a township and became a parish, the spread of work opportunities was underway, but for many the way of life of their forefathers existed largely unchanged until the great social revolution brought about by the First World War.

MILLING

The milling of corn into flour is one of the bases of the English rural economy, and has been carried on for centuries. The earliest reference to the activity in Parbold is from 1288, when two mills in Parbold are recorded.[124] The continuity of the activity can be recognised down through the centuries.

Initially, milling must have been carried out by hand, and would have been a domestic activity. Mechanisation made use first of water power, and in the Parbold area wind power was not employed until the eighteenth century. The sites of two water mills are positively known, one being on a small stream just below Fairhurst Hall, the other being on the River Douglas between the bridge and the canal aqueduct. Both are shown on Yates' Map of Lancashire (1786). A third possible site, in the Fairy Glen, is not shown by Yates, nor has positive evidence of its existence been found.

Parbold Mill is recorded in various documents from the sixteenth,[125] seventeenth [126] and eighteenth centuries. The water mill by the Douglas was generally known as Douglas Mill. It was still standing at about 1875, although in a ruinous state. The mill was a stone built structure.

The equipment used can be accurately identified from an inventory taken in 1723.[127] The following was recorded:

Two chests	fourteen mill picks	a mill saddle
an iron cross	a chisel	lead weights
a piece of iron for letting down the stone		two mill sieves
a dusting sieve	a half bushel measure	a peck measure
a pair of weights or scales		a grater
a ladder	a pair of scales	

The items were valued, in total, at £3 8*s.* 5½ *d.*

Douglas Mill was leased in June 1759 [128] by Mary Crisp, the widow of Thomas Crisp of Parbold Hall, and her daughter Mary, to Samuel Rigby for three lives, those of William Culshaw and the sons of Samuel Rigby, Samuel Junior and Seth. The sons were then aged twenty-one and nineteen respectively. The payment was £100, and a yearly rental of £2 payable at Pentecost and Martinmas. Additionally, all corn for the manor house was to be kiln dried and milled free of charge. The lease covered the water corn mill, a drying kiln, a turf house, and all water courses, dams and so on.

Samuel Rigby soon ran into financial problems, and between 1759 and 1763 a series of mortgages were taken out.[129] In October 1759 the mill was made over to William Lee of Lathom for £30 for ninety-nine years or the life of the longest survivor of the lease. In February 1762 [130] Rigby paid off Lee by making the mill over to Thomas Glover for £55, £32 of which were used to pay off Lee, including interest, and the balance being loaned to Rigby. In turn, the mill was assigned to Robert Sephton of Welch Whittle in 1763 for £120, the balance after paying off Glover being loaned to Rigby. By 1767 the outstanding debt to Sephton amounted to £128, and in September John Tunstall acquired the mill for £253.

John Tunstall died without making a will, and with debts exceeding £270, the main creditors being Thomas Hailcroft of Newburgh, John Hodges of Bispham and Richard Weenall, late of Mawdesley. He left a wife, Ellen, an eldest son, Nathan and several younger children. John Tunstall held lands in Bispham which passed to Nathan, but were administered by his mother until he came of age. Ellen Tunstall acquired further debts, to James Spencer of Newburgh (£46) and Catherine Wright of Ormskirk (£10). She then married James Culshaw, who took on her debts on marriage. Presumably, Ellen Tunstall must have been some woman to have found a husband under such circumstances. Family disputes arose, and Nathan Tunstall considered taking action against James Culshaw and his mother for a bill to sell the mill and have the money raised applied in exoneration of the freehold estates passed on to him. On the intervention of friends the arguments were settled, and it was agreed that the mill should be sold, and the money used to discharge John Tunstall's debts, but Nathan Tunstall should at the same time release all debts against James Culshaw.

The mill was offered for sale at the *Eagle and Child* (now Derby House Saddlery) in Newburgh. After lively bidding it was sold to John Prescott, inn-keeper of Bispham, for £182. Subsequently, Nathan Tunstall agreed with John Prescott to buy the mill by private treaty for the same sum. At the time the mill was in the occupancy of George Bennett, tenant farmer.[131]

The windmill was built some time about 1794 to replace the water mill. Both were advertised for sale by auction at six o'clock in the evening on Wednesday, 2 July 1817, the auction to be held at the house of William Hailwood, 'The Sign of the Mill' in Parbold, near Newburgh.[132] Nathan Tunstall was the owner, and the water mill was still held for the life of Seth Rigby, who was by now aged seventy-six. The yearly quit rent was forty shillings. The water mill was advertised with two pairs of stones, one being adapted for shealing, and the other for grinding oats.

The water mill was still standing in 1829, when an inventory of the machinery and its condition was made by one William Chew. He valued the machinery at £86 14*s.* 8*d.*[133]

The wind mill was known as Nathan's Mill, and was to be sold complete with all the machinery, the warehouse and a plot of land. The mill contained two pairs of French stones, and two pairs of grey stones, as well as three sets of beams and weights. The chief rent was £2 2*s.* 6*d.*

In its turn, the wind mill was to be replaced by the steam driven corn mill on the opposite side of the canal built by Hugh Ainscough in the mid-nineteenth century. Hugh Ainscough was born on a sixty-acre farm at Ulnes Walton in 1816. It was originally intended that he should become a doctor, but at the age of twenty-one he took over a grocery business in Parbold, as well as the wind mill.[134] There was plenty of local corn to grind and the business expanded. Imported corn from America could be loaded direct into barges in Liverpool and brought down the canal for milling. High Ainscough built both Newburgh Mill in Parbold and later, the mill in Burscough to cater for this trade. By 1860 Hugh had been joined in the business by his brother Richard, and the firm became H. and R. Ainscough, continuing trading under this name until relatively recently.

QUARRYING

Quarrying has a long history in the Parbold area. In a document of 1651,[135] William Hawett was described as 'Gent of the Delph, Parbold.' Which delph this refers to is uncertain, although it may well be Delph House in the Fairy Glen. However, the use of the term delph strongly suggests that quarrying was active at that time. Similarly, the existence of a number of late seventeenth-century houses in the district built of local stone would indicate a small quarrying industry.

The development of the Douglas Navigation between 1720 and 1742, and the Leeds and Liverpool Canal towards the end of the eighteenth century, not only provided a ready market for local stone for building locks and lining banks, but also furnished the opportunity for stone to be transported to more distant markets. Previously, the difficulties of transporting a heavy low-value material like stone over

PARTICULARS and CONDITIONS of SALE

OF A MOST DESIRABLE

FREEHOLD ESTATE,

Situate in the Townships of

Parbold, Wrightington, Newborough and *Dalton*,

In the County of LANCASTER,

Heretofore the ESTATE of THOMAS CRISPE, Esq.

CONSISTING OF

The MANOR of PARBOLD,

WITH

The Rights, Royalties, Quit-Rents, and Appurtenances thereto belonging;

A MANSION HOUSE, called PARBOLD HALL,

Built not long since, of the celebrated PARBOLD STONE, situated on an Eminence, and commanding delightful and extensive Prospects over a beautiful and healthy Country;

GARDENS, AND DEMESNE LANDS,

SUNDRY ELIGIBLE FARMS and TENEMENTS,

With their necessary Buildings,

Containing together TWELVE HUNDRED and FIFTY-SIX STATUTE ACRES and Upwards of excellent LAND, mostly PASTURE, and MEADOW, and some WOOD LANDS, stored with Game, and abounding in truly VALUABLE MINES, and QUARRIES of COAL, SLATE, and the PARBOLD STONE, celebrated for its Durability, Colour, Hardness, and other excellent Qualities, contiguous to the LEEDS and LIVERPOOL CANAL, which runs through Part of the Estate, and renders the same of great increasing Value.

Part of the Estate was formerly let on Leases for Lives, many of which are extinct, and most of the subsisting Lives are very old. The rest is either in Hand, or let to Tenants at Will.

THE WHOLE OF THE ANNUAL VALUE OF

Fourteen Hundred & Thirty-One Pounds and Upwards,

Besides the Profits arising from the STONE QUARRIES, &c.

Which will be SOLD by AUCTION,

BY

Mr. CHRISTIE,

At his GREAT ROOM in PALL MALL,

On *Thursday, June* 24th 1790, at One o'Clock,

IN THREE LOTS.

Advertisement for the sale of the Parbold estate, 1790.

Route of the old tram road in the Fairy Glen, with old stone sleeper blocks.

poor, unmade roads, would have restricted the distance to which stone could be carried. Uses to which Parbold stone was put included the training walls of the Ribble Navigation, Haigh Hall, St James' Church, Wigan, and numerous other projects in the development of Southport and Wigan.

By the middle of the eighteenth century, Parbold stone was well known: when the Parbold estate was put up for sale at Christie's in Pall Mall, the description included 'quarries . . . of the Parbold stone, celebrated for its durability, colour, hardness and other excellent properties'.[136] Stone has been quarried in several other places in the township, not all working the same geological horizon.

Interesting records survive from the nineteenth century for a number of quarries in and around Parbold, which would enable a detailed history of the industry to be undertaken.

Possible route of old tram road to Parbold Quarry. There is no map evidence to support this suggestion.

The account books [137] of the quarry in the Fairy Glen, known as Delf House quarry or Appley Moor Delf, are preserved for the period 1844 to 1860 and yield interesting details of the industry. The quarry produced a wide range of products including ashlar, flags, wallstones, channel stones and paving stones. The accounts provide information on names, numbers employed, wage rates and days employed. In the last quarter of 1844, seven men were employed, who received payment of two shillings per day. On 24 January 1845, the men were paid for the period from 9 September to the end of December 1844, or over four months in arrears. In fact, all the men were left with about four days pay still outstanding for this period.

Days worked, out of a possible 114 days, varied from man to man between 84½ days to 95½ days, and averaged 91½ days, or approximately a 5½ day week. Edward Mawdesley, who worked the most had 18½ days off in just over 16 weeks. The workmen were John Dicconson, John Draper, John Molyneux, James Molyneux, Rick Martland, Edward Mawdesley and Thomas Draper. From about 1850 onwards John Molyneux seems to have had some position of authority: he signed the book regularly for having received money for the men's wages. This rather suggests that he was some kind of foreman, or perhaps he was the one who could write.

Delf House Quarry was owned by Charles Scarisbrick, and probably managed on his behalf by William Hawkeshead Talbot, his agent, who came from a well-known local family engaged mainly in surveying, who kept the accounts between himself and the quarry. It is possible that Talbot ran the quarry as a private activity separate from his estate responsibilities.

It has been suggested [138] that the quarry was possibly worked from underground on the basis that the visible quarry workings are insignificant compared with the substantial nature and expense of the associated tramroad.

The business was generally quite profitable as shown by the

Parbold Quarry.
The workforce at Parbold Quarry, probably at the end of the nineteenth century.

following summary of accounts for an eleven-year period, although profitability could vary wildly from year to year.

year	*turnover*			*profit (loss)*		
	£	*s.*	*d.*	£	*s.*	*d.*
1847	375	1	10	73	12	1
1848	405	18	8	76	4	4
1849	366	17	7	(38	13	9)
1850	556	19	5	194	0	1
1851	409	13	6	(32	19	6)
1852	521	9	10	114	14	4
1853	436	4	9	96	8	4
1854	348	6	11	(22	18	5)
1855	444	18	6	(147	10	3)
1856	512	3	1	(34	16	4)
1857	930	7	5	556	3	0

A number of items may be isolated from the expenditure which help to illustrate the working of the operation.

The quarry used explosives, six pounds being purchased at six pence per pound in January 1845. This was probably made at Ulverston and brought to Parbold along the Rufford branch of the canal from a store at Tarleton.[139]

The blacksmith's bill included six shillings for sixteen iron gears for wagons at four and a half pence each.

The cost of transport on the canal is illustrated by a forty-ton load of pavers, which were delivered to Southport for Charles Scarisbrick at one shilling and sixpence per ton.

Stone from the quarry was transported to the canal by a tramroad, which is shown on the 1846 Ordnance Survey map. Stone sleeper blocks can still be found at several points along most of its length, and other remains include rock cuttings, a small embankment, and an arch under the main Manchester to Southport railway line, indicating that the tramway predated the railway. Where blocks remain *in situ* they are typically three feet apart and offset from each

Canal Wharf.
The old wharf on the canal below Parbold Quarry.

other. The line of the tramroad occupies the present stream bed, the stream having been diverted after the closure of the tramroad. The flash floods of Saturday, 22 August 1987, removed considerable parts of the stream bed, and exposed a number of fish-bellied iron rails still in place and firmly plugged to the stone blocks, or at the part of the tramroad nearest to the quarry, to wooden sleepers made from rough tree trunks or branches. The gauge of the tramroad was approximately three feet.

No information on the cost of building the tramroad has been found, but there is some interesting information on a tramroad at Dawber Delf in Appley Bridge, about half a mile away.[140, 141, 142] This tramroad was probably started in about 1815. By 1822 it was in need of repair, although still not completed. It appears to have been completed before 1828, and is shown on the 1846 map. The costs of building the tramroad were estimated by two surveyors, William Shakeshaft and Mr Robinson, probably in an attempt to assess the cost of construction to the tenant, and thereby to assist in fixing his rent. Shakeshaft arrived at a figure of £600 and Robinson £660. These costs come to about £1,000 per mile, which is very low compared to the cost quoted by Baxter[143] of £1,500 per mile in 1801 and £2,500 in 1826. They may be deliberately so, since Shakeshaft was steward to Sir Thomas Hesketh, the landowner, and probably had a vested interest in under-estimating the costs in order to demonstrate the tenant's ability to pay a high rent.

Customers included several works, such as paint works, townships including Downholland and Halsall, the Southport Commissioners, Greenslate Colliery, the Manchester and Southport Railway and Charles Scarisbrick's estates at Wrightington and Scarisbrick, as well as for building developments being carried out on his land in Wigan and Southport. The Scarisbrick estate was probably the largest customer. Some large orders were received: these included one in 1852 for two thousand tons of paving stones, 1,300 yards of side stones, 1,300 yards of channel stones and a similar quantity of 'stones next to the channel'. This order was for new streets being laid out in Wigan.

Another interesting order was received from Thomas Bimpson in 1848.[144] This was for 296 tons of rough stone at 8*d.* per ton. This

Stone yard.
The stone yard on the canal bank opposite Parbold Windmill.

was delivered in forty- and thirty-ton lots between March and August of that year.

The early history of Parbold Quarry (on Parbold Hill) is less well documented. As we have seen it was well established by 1790 and, since it was listed as a separate property in the Land Tax Assessments, it would be possible to work out the details of ownership and occupiers from that time onwards. It developed into the main quarry in the village and continued working until just a few years ago. It was conveniently placed for both the canal and the railway, and was linked to both by the 1890s by a railway which utilised the weight of the loaded wagons going down the incline to pull the unloaded ones back up the hill to the quarry. There is also physical evidence of a cutting which probably provided a route for an earlier tramroad which may have pre-dated the railway. There is, however, no documentary evidence of this.

Other quarries were working in the nineteenth century on Hunter's Hill, Hawett Hill and at Brandreth Delf. Stone from these quarries probably was loaded on to barges by the windmill bridge, where there was a stone wharf. An agreement was signed on 19 January between Charles Scarisbrick and Robert Blackburn, described as a delfmaster but also running the *Windmill Inn*, to let the wharf north of the canal and on the west side of the Windmill Bridge at an annual rental of £3.[145]

A bye law of the Leeds Liverpool Canal Company required that any goods unloaded on the bank should be placed at least five feet from the bank edge.

Occupation of quarries was often short-lived, the owners frequently seeking fresh tenants. Correspondence between William Hawkeshead Talbot, on behalf of Charles Scarisbrick, and William Cookson of Parbold shows some of the aspects of letting a quarry.[146] In 1846 Cookson agreed terms for renting the quarries as follows:

1. He will open up a road into the hill opposite the house occupied by Hugh Ainscough between now and Candlemas 1848, during which term he will pay no rent.
2. From Candlemas 1848 he will pay fifty pounds per year due in advance for ten labourers. If more men are employed the rent for every man above that number will be four pounds per man.
3. The term will be for seven years from Candlemas 1848.

On 22 February 1847 Talbot sent a note to Cookson to quit the land on the second of February (Candlemas) next, and the house on 12 May following. Cookson agreed to quit in a letter dated 1 February 1848, and a poster survives for a sale of furniture, livestock, farming equipment and delf tools at the house of William Cookson, Parbold on 29 March 1848. The list of quarry tools included a chain, a nearly new crane, a pair of bellows, an anvil, wedges, hammers, picks, drills, spades, etc. The domestic effects provide an impressive list and suggest a reasonable level of affluence. The full list was:

mahogany four post bed and camp beds, feather beds, pillows etc.

clock in oak case	mahogany corner cupboard	
mahogany chest	oak chest	chairs, tables
kitchen dresser	looking glasses	pictures
wine and other glasses	china, tea trays	chimney ornaments
iron oven, grate, boiler	copper kettle	clothes horse
earthenware	kitchen requisites	books

This list gives a picture of a cultured and educated man returning to a home with books, pictures and wine glasses.

Why Cookson had to quit is not known, but the fact that he was selling up would suggest that he may have got into debt.

Re-letting the quarries does not seem to have gone too smoothly. In October 1848 John Robinson was in correspondence with Talbot on his nephew's behalf, making an offer less than Cookson's of two years earlier. This was put forward as a fair offer considering the distance from the canal and the cost of carting making these quarries less competitive than those nearer the canal.

A reply from Talbot said that he had submitted the proposal to Charles Scarisbrick, but they had a rule on the estate of never altering terms once they are fixed, otherwise they would be continually bargaining. This quarry is believed to be the one on Hawett Hill.

COAL MINING

There is evidence of coal mining in Parbold from at least the early 1750s, when Joshua Tunstall, who worked the water mill in Parbold, was paid five shillings to compensate him for trespass on his land

Gillibrand Colliery.
The site of the former Gillibrand Colliery. The trees are located in a hollow, probably the result of mine subsidence.

by the carters taking the coal to the river from John Taylor's coal pits in Parbold.[147] These pits worked a poor quality coal from the field on the right hand side of the road going up Parbold Hill, and shown on the estate maps and tithe map as 'Coal pit Hey'.

Two years later, in 1754, Thomas Crisp signed an agreement for a period of three years with John Taylor and Mathew Smith, both of Haigh, to 'dig, search for, sough, trench and get' all the coal they could from the recently discovered mines between the Blackfields, the Wood Wall and Littlefields in Parbold and Wrightington.[148] It should be noted that the use of the term 'mine' does not necessarily imply the existence of a coal pit, since it is commonly used to mean a coal seam.

The Gillibrand estate was put up for sale by auction in 1767 by William Sale, who had inherited it from Jonathan Gillibrand. Advertised features of the estate [149] included considerable quantities of young growing timber and a valuable coal mine which 'may be got with great advantage by the purchaser as the Douglas Navigation flows through the same by means whereof the coal may be put on board vessels'. There is no indication that the coal was being worked.

John Banks, who will also be mentioned later, was investigating an estate in Parbold in about 1788 to 1790. He sank one pit upon the coal crop, which was about fourteen and a half yards deep, and bored down to the coal reached at forty seven yards. There were two coal seams, the first was two feet thick, the second four feet one inch thick, the two being separated by three feet two inches. An account of borings dated August 1790,[150] and referring specifically to Gillibrands within Parbold, shows two coals at a depth of fifty-five yards, the first being one foot six inches thick, the second four feet and separated by two feet ten inches. This log agrees remarkably well with John Banks'.

This boring was probably made by Thomas Chadwick, since a log dated the tenth of March, referring to borings in Parbold in the Upper Wood is written in the same hand. In 1793, Thomas Chadwick carried out further borings, this time in Hand Lane, near the bridge. This hole was started on the twenty-seventh of May and completed on the tenth of July, and was measured at ninety-four yards six inches, indicating a progress in excess of two yards per day. Borings were also made across the lane above Parbold Wood, again locating the same two coal seams.

By about 1790 there appears, therefore, to have been considerable interest in the development of a colliery at Gillibrands, and further evidence is provided in a letter [151] of 1789, which discusses the possibility of treating with Mr Sale for the development of the colliery, but there is a clear implication that the mine was not then working. It was estimated that coal underlay about twenty-five acres of the estate.

The first indication of the working of the pit is from the Land Tax Assessments of 1796, which show a charge of ten shillings on Mr Sale for the coal pits. A lease for the colliery dated the first of July 1798, exists at Wigan Record Office,[152] but is unfortunately only fragmentary. From this document, however, it seems that the colliery was originally leased by James Sale the Elder to Jonathan Sale, Rylands Sale and James Sale the Younger, who opened the colliery in 1796. In January 1798 the Sales went bankrupt and assigned the colliery to Michael Harrison, coal merchant of Newburgh, and Henry Ellam, coal merchant, of Standish. The lease of July of that year was for John Clarke to take over and work the mine. Presumably Harrison and Ellam lacked the resources. Henry Ellam was an experienced mine manager, having been with Blundell's Collieries in Orrell, and coming from a family of colliery agents in the St Helens area. He would not, therefore, be lacking in technical knowledge. There must have been drainage problems: the lease refers specifically to Clarke deepening the present engine shaft by ten yards, and driving tunnels in such a way that the engine already erected could drain and carry off the water. Provision was made for Clarke to improve the engine or erect a more powerful one if necessary. The nature of the engine is not stated, but it may well have been a Newcomen type atmospheric engine, since such engines were being used locally, and Clarke himself was using them in his Orrell mines.[153]

John Clarke, born about 1756, was the younger son of William Clarke, who founded Clarke's Bank, the first bank to be established in Liverpool. He had considerable mining interests in Orrell. The banking side of his business went bankrupt in 1816, but Clarke's personal fortune was estimated at that time as over £100,000. He would, therefore, have brought to Gillibrands both technical and financial resources.

Two maps [154] shed further light on the workings of the colliery. The first, on a scale of thirty-two yards to one inch, shows the location of the four shafts and associated surface buildings in relation to the canal, Gillibrands House and Wood Lane. The down dip shaft is called the engine shaft, and is located close to a basin off the canal, presumably used for loading coal. The map is undated, but refers to surrounding land as belonging to Edward Dicconson. It therefore relates to after 1800, when he inherited, but prior to 1807, when he died.

The second plan shows details of the underground workings, and allows accurate dating of the main period of working, since an annotation states that a fault was encountered on the 22f March 1799, and John Banks went to Standish to inform Henry Ellam, and John Brown told Mr Michael Harrison on 8 April. From this plan an estimate of the amount of coal extracted during the working of the colliery seems to be about 14,000 tons net.[155] The main period of working was before 1800, and there is no evidence of the colliery on the Gillibrand estate map of 1809, the field in that area being called Great Marl'd Earth.

A third, and more important mine, was Parbold Colliery, located on the north side of the main road over Parbold Hill, towards High Moor. This mine worked in the first half of the nineteenth century. In September 1815, Mr Whittle, of Charnock Richard, wrote to William Shakeshaft concerning a visit he had made to Parbold Colliery, and commenting that Walker, who ran the pit, must be losing money daily on the venture, the coal being thin and of poor quality.[156] William Shakeshaft was Sir Thomas Hesketh's agent, the colliery being on Hesketh land. The following year a new road was constructed to the colliery, but Walker withdrew from the venture. An inventory lists the items left behind at the collieries by him as:

two whimseys	two wood baskets	one pair bellows
two ropes	two sinking hoppets	one anvil
two iron pullies	two water tubs	one sinking pail
six sheds	one banking barrow	two brow hooks
one turn with headgear and one rope		two wood pullies
thirteen whiskets	one box barrow	six scaffold board

one coal spade	twenty baskets slack	ten baskets coal
one cabbin		

A note dated March 1816 implies that Walker only scratched the surface, one of the workmen having asserted that all the best coal is still to be got, and that one man should be able to get sixteen to twenty baskets a day, and that there ought to be seven or eight galleries in use at one time. In the spring of that year a new road was constructed to the colliery. Parbold Colliery was active in the period from 1827 to 1830, from which period a number of papers survive.[157]

In 1829 there were ten workers, and in the following year thirteen colliers were employed. In 1829 the miners were paid at 2½ *d.* per basket for coal, and 1½ *d.* for slack. Baskets varied in size, but in the latter part of the eighteenth century were about 120–150 pounds in weight.[158] In September 1829 wages varied for the ten workers from 4*s.* 3*d.* to 13*s.* 4*d.* Production appears to have been about three baskets of coal for every basket of slack, and about three tons of coal were typically produced each day.

A rough calculation of costs includes the following information:

	s.	*d.*
getting	2	11
winding		2
carting		10
cleaning and loading		3
river (canal?) dues	2	4
unloading		3
yard rent		2
	6	11
profit	3	–

Information from elsewhere in the records suggests a selling price of 5*d.* a basket, which would indicate that the baskets were probably about one hundred pounds in weight. The above calculation was worked out by whoever did it in 1830 on the assumption that they could produce about twenty tons per day, or three boat loads per week, which does not seem to agree with the actual production for the periods checked, but probably reflects the perrenial optimism of miners. During this period development work was carried out, with an agreement for sinking sixteen yards of shaft at 18*s*. per yard, and among items bought were over 10,000 bricks, spades, ropes, buckets, baskets, trams etc. The carpenter's bill for 1828 [159] included £28 5*s*. for a small gin wheel for winding coal. Sales were made both to Liverpool and to 'the Country'.

Just when Parbold Colliery ceased to function is uncertain. On the tithe map of 1837 it is described as 'old coal pit'. However, a paper, apparently dated 1866, refers to the loading of boats from Alder Lane with thirty-six ton loads of both coal and slack.

POTTERY MANUFACTURE

A stoneware pottery was working in Parbold early in the nineteenth century, and possibly at the end of the eighteenth. This was located near Chapel House on the Chapel Flatt and The Tag, on the north side of the canal.

In 1802 [160] a lease was drawn up between Edward Dicconson and John Rylands, linen manufacturer of Wigan, for two closes of land called Chapel Flatt and The Tag, totalling between one and two acres, together with several buildings then used for the manufacture of earthenware. The pottery had formerly been in the possession of Henry Meadows.

By 1808 the pottery was being run by Andrew Henderson, who had taken it over from someone called Dean.[161] Henderson claimed that when he took it over the works were in a ruinous state, and that its reputation was such that few retailers would sell the ware and few purchasers buy it. However, by persistance in seeking sales and attention to detail the reputation had been built up, and by 1808 the ware was considered, even in Liverpool, to be as good as any made in the county. It was, however, necessary to carefully remove the organic fibres and decayed roots which were present in the pot clay.

Henderson appears to have been progressive, and had carried out experiments to prove that he could make quality stoneware, jars and bottles equal to Chesterfield ware, which in view of the expensive land carriage to Liverpool was an important consideration. Henderson claimed to have spent over £500 on the works, as a result of which he was short of funds. In the summer and autumn of 1808 he was attempting to raise capital from Thomas Eccleston of Scarisbrick Hall. He was hoping to convert his present stable and warehouse into a workshop, and to build a new kiln and new accommodation for his workmen. The latter was required to house his present workforce who had come from Prescot and Warrington, and who had experienced difficulty in finding accommodation.

Henderson also hoped to use the accommodation to attract workers from Chesterfield, hopefully by Christmas that year. The pottery worked shifts, and another reason for wanting accommodation on site was that at shift turnovers the kiln could be left unattended, with a consequent exposure to fire risk, while the workers went to Newburgh or Gillibrands to find their reliefs. Henderson required a few hundred pounds for the immediate needs, but hoped that if things went well, then Mr Eccleston would help in building him a house at the pottery and a road along the canal to Owler's Lane (now Alder Lane) Bridge.

Henderson's detailed proposals to Eccleston were:

1. If Eccleston would build the new premises, Henderson would pay seven per cent for money expended on the new buildings, and a lower percentage on the existing buildings. This was in addition to the current tenancy.
2. Alternatively, if Henderson could get a twenty-one year lease at the present rent, he would build at his own expense a large warehouse, stables for five horses, a kiln and at least three cottages, and he would keep these and the present buildings in good repair.

Although Henderson maintained that he had clay which would enable him to rival the Chesterfield product, and that clay from Prescot was inferior to his in its glazing properties, at some time he had difficulty in obtaining local supplies since he solicited Eccleston's help in getting permission to extract clay from a Mr Draper's land. The clay was to be extracted by ditching, and Draper, the tenant, would welcome it if the landlord, Colonel Stanley, would agree. Failure to get this clay would, according to Henderson, require shutting the pottery down for at least a week while negotiations were made to get material from Prescot. Usuages were said to be about five cubic yards *per annum*.

Accounts submitted in August 1809 showed that the pottery had purchased 25¾ cubic yards of fireclay at 1*s*. 10*d*. per yard, and 75 cubic yards of pot clay at 1*s*. 4*d*. per yard. The latter material had been obtained from Parbold Wood.

Whether Henderson was successful in raising money is not known. Thomas Eccleston died in 1809, and by 1813 [162] a lease for letting the house, outbuildings, stable and two crofts was drawn up with Francis, or Frank, Holme. This seems to have fallen through, and in 1815–16 negotiations were taking place with John Greener, of the family from Chapel House, for the renting of premises consisting of a house, outbuildings, two pottery cottages, various other cottages and meadows, wood, land and other items constituting, in all, over twenty-four acres. From that time onwards there appear to be no further references to the pottery in Parbold.

BRICKMAKING

The traditional building material of the district—stone from the local quarries—was at some time superseded by bricks. Gillibrand's house was faced with bricks, probably in the late eighteenth century, although where they were made is not known. Bricks from some of the demolished outbuildings at Gillibrand's were very uneven, and containing numerous pebbles, suggesting that they were made from local boulder clay.

In 1857 H. and R. Ainscough wrote from their new mill in Parbold, although known as Newburgh Mill, to Hawkshead Talbot, Charles Scarisbrick's agent, concerning brickmaking.[163] They had found a bed of clay on the land formerly occupied by William Bullen and were seeking permission to make some bricks from it for their own use, but not for sale, and would make good the land after taking the clay. Permission was granted at a price of one shilling per cubic yard or three shillings per thousand bricks.

Commercial brickmaking seems to have started in Parbold in about 1860 on the land between Wood Lane and the railway and behind the present-day Atherton's Garage. John Cartmel, who was described as a farmer, shipbuilder and ship owner, had taken over this land and added it to the other land and house he was leasing from Charles Scarisbrick.

The area was in a very rough and ready state, and he improved it by drainage, filling in some of the pits, and by taking down some old fences. At Candlemas 1860 two fields totalling about three Cheshire acres were taken over by Platt and Magnall, brickmakers. Cartmel was paid £10 per acre compensation per year until 1863, when he was awarded £30 in final compensation.[164] This seems to have been remarkably generous, since he was only leasing the land from year to year.[165]

Platt and Magnall remained in business on this site until about 1916. The 1893 25-inch Ordnance Survey map shows a long conveyor or tramroad to the quarrying area, and a second incline or tramroad to a siding on the Lancashire and Yorkshire railway. By 1907 [166] this second incline was extended to the canal, and a further incline ran to a new quarrying area south of the railway, where the recent land fill (1988) has been taking place. The activities on the siding, and the transportation of bricks by rail, are recorded in some of the railway papers.[167]

In 1871 a Francis Young, born in Neath, South Wales, was recorded in the census as a brickmaker employing forty-one men and five boys, and was presumably managing the brickworks in Parbold. Later the labour force seems to have been about twenty-five, including some children.[168] Bricks were used locally in the expansion of the village following the arrival of the railway, such as in the development of Station Road in the 1870s.

BASKETMAKING

Industry in general, and agriculture and the extractive industries in particular, required containers in which to carry their produce. The common container used for this purpose until this century was the wicker-work basket made from willow. Indeed, in industries such as the coal industry, the 'basket' was the commonly used measure of output.

It is said that basketmaking was carried out in every county in the country.[169] However, there were three areas in England where osier beds, where willows were grown, were particularly notable, and consequently basketmaking was especially active. These were the Trent Valley, Somerset, and the district within a ten-mile radius of Mawdesley. Indeed, within this area the tradition has been maintained until recent times. Early maps of Parbold show the presence of osier beds along the Douglas.

5

The Modern Village

THE last hundred years marks a convenient period to consider as that of the modern village. This period more or less coincides with the change in status of Parbold from a township in the parish of Eccleston to that of a civil parish in its own right following the Local Government Act 1894. This period has also seen greater changes in the village than had previously taken place since the earliest records were made, and moreover these changes are correspondingly better documented. Consequently it would be possible to write a history of the last hundred years at much greater length than for earlier centuries. This is not the intention, and this chapter is merely a dip into selected aspects of the modern village. The period of the modern village, therefore, offers the greatest scope for further research.

Whilst Parbold is clearly identifiable as a physical entity, its wider allegiances and associations in modern times are less clear. Throughout most of the last hundred years it has been administered as part of the Wigan Rural District Council, within the County of Lancashire. Since 1974 it has come within the jurisdiction of the West Lancashire District Council, but still within the shire county of Lancashire. At the turn of the century, mail was received via Southport, whilst now the postal address is Wigan. The village has in the past appeared in both Wigan and Southport district directories (a good source of local history information). Within recent times the Member of Parliament has been from the Westhoughton constituency, an area without any apparent link to Parbold, and now the village is represented at Westminster by the member for Chorley. Local events are reported in both the *Wigan Observer* and the *Ormskirk Advertiser*.

Now that the majority of people work outside the village, and have in many instances only lived within the village for a relatively short time, local allegiances are probably even less clear and less strong than they were at the beginning of the present century, when the majority of the population were probably of local origin.

LOCAL NEWS

The local papers provide a continuous record of the day-to-day events throughout the district, both the *Ormskirk Advertiser* and the *Wigan Observer* having been established well before the period here being considered. The local newspapers in the late-nineteenth century, although reporting some local news, were predominantly filled with national and international items. The styles were austere: no photographs, virtually no headlines, and close-packed columns of small print. In the early 1900s occasional photographs began to appear in the *Ormskirk Advertiser*, the first regular use appearing in mid-1918, with excellent photographs of the war. This, however, was almost certainly not a local production, but a 'syndicated' supplement produced nationally and distributed through local papers. By the late 1930s, news reported was almost entirely local, the use of photographs was widespread, and with the exception of the front page, which was still advertisements, a relatively modern format had been adopted.

As only a small part of the areas served by the local papers, Parbold figures infrequently in their columns, maybe two or three times a year, unless some particular event has been deemed worthy of reporting. Generally such news is little more than a catalogue of births, marriages and deaths, news of local worthies, local sports, shows and special events, and if the reporter was particularly lucky, a minor local catastrophe or scandal.

The sending of Thomas Whalley Rhodes to gaol in 1940 must have been such a minor local news item. Rhodes was a farmer at Chapel House Farm when he was brought before the magistrates at Standish for working a horse in an unfit state, and for beating the animal with a wire. A number of witnesses and the RSPCA inspector provided graphic accounts of the incident, which resulted in Rhodes being sentenced to one month's hard labour on both charges, the sentences to run concurrently.[170]

At the end of the nineteenth century there seems to have been a particular spate of railway accidents reported in the *Ormskirk*

Advertiser, not only in Parbold, but at several nearby places, including Rainford Junction, Kirkby and Birkdale. In December 1896 the inquest took place at the *Railway Hotel*, Parbold, on a collier from Wigan. He and a friend had been drinking heavily in Standish, and during the course of the evening they decided to walk to Rufford to go poaching rabbits. While walking along the railway line in the neighbourhood of Parbold Station, one of them was fatally struck by a train.[171]

An even more bizarre and sad accident took place at Parbold station the following February. Robert Leach, a thirty-six year old district councillor living in Newburgh, set off to catch the train to Wigan. As he approached the station, the level crossing gates were closed, and the Wigan train was already in the station. Leach thereupon ran for the train and climbed over the gate (at this time there was no subway), but was hit a glancing blow by a Wigan to Southport train coming into the station. He died some forty-five minutes later.[172]

A further tragic railway accident occured in 1939, when a fourteen-year old girl fell from an express train from Southport as it sped through Parbold Station at about sixty miles per hour. She was returning with her family from a day out at Southport, and was standing by the window when the door opened and she fell out.

The First World War saw the reduction in the reporting of local sports and social news, and the *Ormskirk Advertiser* was filled primarily with farming and war news only. By 1917, when fighting on the Western Front was at its height, the columns regularly contained lists of local casualties. The *Wigan Observer* contained a regular picture gallery of photographs of the fallen. A particular tribute in the *Advertiser* was to Private Tom Lindsay of Parbold and the King's Liverpool Regiment, who was killed in action. This was a long and most glowing tribute from his commanding officer, who led the attack in which Private Lindsay was killed, to his parents, and was certainly far more than the necessary duty letter. Other Parbold casualties reported included James Rigby, formerly the Parbold postman, killed in action; Corporal Frank Briggs, who before the war was the Parbold scoutmaster, and who was severely wounded and had his right leg amputated; Lieutenant Ronald Reay, who was an old boy of Wigan grammar school, and had been promoted from the ranks, was killed in 1918, having previously survived a gas attack and being wounded the previous November. In all, Parbold lost fifteen men in the First World War, seven officers and eight private soldiers. At a vestry meeting held in April 1919, the erection of a war memorial was discussed, but no decision as to what form it should take was made.[173] Ultimately it was decided that a plaque should be put up in the church, and this was dedicated by the Bishop of Manchester in May 1920. Parbold is thus one of the few places in the country without a traditional war memorial erected after the First World War.

LOCAL AFFAIRS

Following the Local Government Act of 1894 and the establishment of Parbold as a civil parish, it became necessary to elect a parish council. On 4 December 1894 the first parish meeting was held with this purpose in mind. About fifty-five people attended, and the meeting must have ended in some excitement, because following an original election by a show of hands, an objection was lodged, and a poll demanded by Mr James Welding. The newly-elected council met for the first time on 7 January 1895, and one of the first actions was the placing of an order for the purchase of a parish seal costing £1 2*s.* 6*d.*

The minutes of the parish council provide an interesting account of local events both relatively major (in local terms) and trivial, and also demonstrate the slowness with which progress may be made.[174] Some of the items which were discussed in the early years have a familiar ring today. Among these may be included the forerunner of the 'Parbold Pong' and the library.

The Act of Parliament which established Parbold as a civil parish, also set up district councils. Parbold came under the control of Wigan Rural District Council. This basically took over the role of the previously existing Rural Sanitary Authority of the Wigan Union, who met in the boardroom of Wigan Workshouse in King Street. Local parochial committees also existed for all the townships within the Wigan Union and continued under the Rural District Council until they were finally disbanded in 1954. Minute books of the Rural Sanitary Authority exist from 1872,[175] as do the minute books of the Rural District Council [176] and the Parbold Parochial Committee.[177] They all provide interesting information on local affairs. The main responsibilities of the District Council concerned public health and water supply.

Complaints about the smells emanating from the Hoscar sewage farm were first recorded in 1896. This sewage works was operated by Wigan Corporation, another local authority but without any direct control over Parbold. The result of an inspection in 1896 suggested that the smell was not coming from the works, but was the result of Parbold's own sewage being discharged directly into the Douglas without treatment along an open and stagnant ditch which was bubbling with gases of decomposition. Parbold did not have a satisfactory sewage disposal scheme at this time, and schemes were put forward in 1899 and 1900 to deal with it. However, this suggestion that the smell was due entirely to local sewage does not seem to have stood the test of time.

Complaints to Wigan Corporation were frequent thereafter. In 1913 the smell was particularly strong, and Mr J. H. Wilson, the local Medical Officer of Health was moved to write to the members of the Rural District Council as follows:

> I have again to complain very strongly about the nuisance to which the residents of the Township of Parbold are subjected by reason of the stench from the Wigan Corporation Sewerage situated about a mile and a half to the west at Hoscar.
>
> For some months the smell has been less noticeable but about three weeks ago, that is about the second week in June, it became so noticeable as to be the subject of comment and complaint. Since this time it has grown in intensity until on Wednesday evening last (July 2nd) it became absolutely unbearable; those sitting out of doors had to take refuge inside, and those indoors had to close all means of ingress by closing doors and windows.
>
> The odour is of an intensely nauseating nature such as one might expect from the release of pent up sewage.
>
> This matter is becoming a serious menace to the property as well as the health of Parbold; many who in former years used to go there in the summer months are avoiding the place, whilst some of the residents aver that its continuance will entail their leaving the district.
>
> Very strong representations should be made as to its seriousness

> to the Corporation of the Borough of Wigan and if necessary legal action taken to enable the people of Parbold to live in comfort and freedom from this now almost intolerable nuisance.

Correspondence between the two local authorities continued over the years without any resolution of the problem.

In 1923 the Clerk to the Parish Council was instructed to write to Wigan Rural District Council, and state that in the opinion of the Council the nuisance arising from the sewage works at Hoscar is worse than for many years and that it appears to be getting worse each year. Wigan Rural District Council was requested to enquire of Wigan Corporation if they were taking any and what steps to improve the system. The reply was that the corporation could 'not admit that any nuisance arises'.

The library was another long running saga. Proposals for a library were first recorded in 1901, and raised at subsequent intervals, but only finally realised with the opening of the new library in 1989.

In 1909 a letter was received by the parish council from the Leyland Gas Company enquiring what the council would be willing to contribute for a gas supply to be laid on to the village—another proposal which again would only be realised some eighty years or so later.

Parbold has generally been slow to gain the benefits of public utilities. A mains water supply was inaugurated on 4 October 1894, just before the parish council came into being. The reservoir was located above the present-day Parbold Douglas school, there being sufficient head to supply the bulk of the village, and was fed by a spring without pumping. The inflow was measured at 11,500 gallons per day, and the assumption was made that seven gallons were required per day per head of population. With a population of six hundred and thirty the actual requirements per day were about 4,500 gallons, thus giving a supply in excess of the need at that time. The cost of the scheme was £1,300. Following the opening ceremony the official party retired to the Coach House in Brandreth Delf for refreshments.

The reservoir's location behind the current school meant it could not supply properties further up the hill, the majority of which were on the Parbold estate. This fact was brought to the attention of the Rural District Council, who were requested to write to the Hon.

Gerard Dicconson, the owner of the estate, to compel him to provide a supply. A report of all property without water was to be made.

By 1921 the original supply was beginning to be considered inadequate. The bore was 3½ inches in diameter, and the well 34 feet deep. An expert from Bath inspected the supply, and considered that an 8-inch diameter bore driven to 50 feet would increase the supply, which he had measured at 11,000 gallons per day, by fifty per cent. There were problems with the original contractor taken on to do the job, who lost his drill bit and could not afford to recover it.

Concern arose again in 1930 about the adequacy of the supply, a geological consultant being instructed to prepare a report. At this time the daily yield was averaging 36,000 gallons per day, but at the lowest flow, in drought conditions, was only just able to meet the demand. Consumption at this time was between twenty-three and twenty-four gallons per head per day. The more than threefold increase in consumption per person per day since 1894 may be taken as a measure of the improvement in general living standards.

In 1910 an offer was made to lay down a public electric light supply to the village. A small works would be set up in the district, and electric mains would be carried along the side of the roads on wooden or light steel poles. They could also be used to carry a street light on a small bracket. Although the council elected to look into the scheme further, nothing came of it. However, street lighting remained an issue, and in 1927 and 1928 long discussions were held over the idea of using oil lamps to light the approaches to the canal bridge in Mill Lane following a fatality. Then in 1930 the Clerk to the Council was instructed to write to the Lancashire Electricty Power Company in Manchester to arrange an appointment to obtain information on the costs of lighting the roads in the village. In the same year a request was made to the General Post Office for a telephone kiosk to be erected in the village.

Road safety was another recurring theme. In 1895 the Cyclist Touring Club (CTC) gained approval to erect a warning notice on Parbold Hill, and in 1898 there was council support for a by-law compelling all vehicles to carry lights when travelling after sunset. In 1897 a request was made, on safety grounds, to the Lancashire and Yorkshire Railway Company for a passenger subway by the level crossing in the village, but a further six years were to pass before the railway company was persuaded to start the work. In 1921 concern was expressed over the nuisance caused by cars coming from the Vulcan Works at Crossens, and also motor cyclists who came to test their machines on Parbold Hill. The actual condition of the road between the railway and canal bridges in Alder Lane was cause for concern in 1898, it being considered to be dangerous.

The Medical Officer of Health reported on the births and deaths in Parbold quarterly, and also upon outbreaks of contagious diseases. The overall improvement in public health is evident from the decrease in the latter, outbreaks being fairly frequent early in this century. For example, in 1912 there were six cases of scarlet fever in the village, one of which proved fatal. In the same year an outbreak of measles closed both the Catholic and Church of England schools. Drownings, too, seemed to have been not infrequent occurences, presumably from falling into the canal. They may also reflect a less general ability to swim compared to today.

The nineteenth-century growth of urban areas such as Liverpool led to an increasing problem of the disposal of refuse. The canal provided a convenient way of getting refuse away from the urban communities, and a number of places in Parbold alongside the canal at which nineteenth-century bottles and ceramic jam and paste jars can be found bear witness to this activity. In 1893 the nuisance arising from the dumping of refuse from Bootle at Gillibrand was considered by the Parbold Parochial Committee and referred to the rural council to see whether an action to restrain the occupier of the land or the contractor from dumping could be obtained. The Gillibrand site seems to have continued for quite some time. In 1935 the *Wigan Observer* reported a lengthy discussion on tipping at Gillibrands. There were complaints about rats, the smell, and dangers to health. Councillor Hampson was quoted as saying ‘it seems grossly unfair that a city’s rubbish should be tipped in our district’. A sentiment very similar to that expressed in more recent times with the proposal to dump Manchester’s waste in Parbold quarry, and which is currently taking place.

On a more local level, concern was expressed at the district council in 1896 about the need for a system for emptying the local ashpits and cesspools. In 1898 James Turner, a local farmer, appeared before the council when his offer to empty the privvies and ashpits in Parbold for £10 (subject to the provision by the council of a suitable tip) was accepted. In 1915 the tip was located in Tanhouse Lane, a complaint being made about the nuisance being caused by flies. In the same year a proposal was discussed for the provision of bins to replace the ashpits then in use.

Among cargoes carried on the canal, manure was not uncommon, which on unloading could be left on the canal banks and wharfs, leading to complaints and orders that it should be removed within a limited time period in order to reduce the smell.

DECAY AND RENEWAL

Parbold at the turn of the century was clearly a place both different and yet similar to what it is today. The 'Parbold Pong' was a current issue then as it is now, and the village was then as now a dumping ground for the refuse of a distant conurbation. However, to add to these problems, the roads were poorly made, many houses insanitary, the streets unlit, the water supply barely adequate, and epidemics not infrequent. Parbold had its own 'clochmerle', which led in 1898 to a request to the parish council for the removal of the urinal in front of the Mill House Inn because it was indecent. This was clearly done, but despite a recommendation for the provision of a public convenience (a site was suggested near the end of Beech Avenue), Parbold still remains without this basic public facility.

By 1915 the beacon on the top of Parbold Hill was said to be falling down, as was the drinking fountain at the bottom of Tanhouse Lane which had been erected to commemorate Queen Victoria's Jubilee. It was made of Burnley stone and had only been unveiled in 1898. The fountain was removed, lost, rediscovered, and finally restored and re-sited outside the new library in 1989. The beacon took some time to repair: a request was made for its repair in 1931, but nothing was done. It was finally blown down by a storm in 1942, and remained nothing but a pile of stones until it was finally restored in 1958. Photographs of the bottle taken just before the Second World War show it to have been a much bigger structure than the current monument. It is also said to have been rebuilt in a slightly different place.

Whilst we can only imagine the physical appearance of Parbold in earlier centuries, the last hundred years have been recorded, to a greater or lesser extent, in photographs, giving a more concrete image of the development of the village.[178]

By 1917 it was reported that there were a number of houses in Parbold which under normal conditions would have been closed as unfit for human habitation. However, all the existing houses in the village were occupied, giving rise to overcrowding, and the Rural District Council considered that twelve extra houses for the working classes were required. By 1919 this estimate had risen to forty to meet the requirements of employees at the flour mill, boat yard and quarries.

The nineteenth century had seen the progressive decrease in the numbers employed in farming, and the development of local industries, and the establishment of local shops. The inter-war years saw a period of unemployment, and a number of schemes were initiated to alleviate its affects. These included negotiations between the owner of Parbold Hall and the Order of Friends to purchase the Hall to set up a colony for the unemployed. Similar schemes were operated by the Catholic Land Association at Priorswood Hall, where a 'back to the land' scheme, catering for up to five hundred men was seen as the only solution to unemployment.

The later years of the twentieth century have seen the gradual disappearance of local employment, and the change of Parbold into a dormitory area with the majority of people travelling out of the village to work everyday.

The last boat was launched at the boatyard in 1926, although the yard did not finally close until the 1940s. Life in the boatyard has been recorded by Harry Leyland.[179] A days work was from six in the morning until five-thirty at night, with a six-day week and no paid holidays. After an eight-year apprenticeship, wages were £2 14*s*. a week. During the 1930s the canal trade was in decline and the competition from neighbouring yards at Burscough and Wigan frequently led to the workers being laid off.

Parbold Hall was empty by the mid-1950s and badly in need of repair.[180] It was rescued from further decay in 1958 when it was purchased by Peter Moores, the current owner, and restored.

From a population of just over 600 in 1891, Parbold has grown to a large village of over 3,000 people. Until 1960 this growth was steady, but during the 1960s and 1970s growth was rapid with the infilling with new housing estates of various open areas within the village. Later developments have generally been smaller in scale, and providing luxury houses at the top end of the market. These have included the development of the disused Brandreth Delf Quarry as a luxury housing complex, and the conversion into homes of a number of derelict barns in the district.

More recently a large number of dwellings has been added to the village housing stock with the redevelopment of the site of the former mill. However, the character of Parbold could have been very different from what it is today had the original proposals of the county council in 1948 to make Parbold one of three new towns to cope with urban overspill gone ahead.[181] The proposal met with bitter opposition locally, and although Parbold was considered to be a superior location, the proposed site was changed to Skelmersdale.

LEISURE

The late nineteenth and early twentieth centuries saw an increasing amount of time for leisure, which, without the availability of mass entertainment characteristic of the second half of the twentieth century, led to an increase in the number of local societies. They included agricultural and floral societies, a brass band and the Parbold Social Club.

The Parbold Social Club was the venue for many local meetings, such as the parish council. It was founded in December 1893 following a public meeting held at the Windmill Inn clubroom. The meeting had been called by Mr Threlfall, chairman of the parochial committee, and was well attended, and in full agreement to form a social club, apart from one individual who had had rather too much to drink. A room to use as a clubroom was offered by Ainscoughs, and a committee was elected. The club was to be non-political, non-sectarian, and without intoxicating liquor, but Mr Threlfall, the chairman, hoped it would continue to serve the local community for many years. His hopes seem to have been realised. The gentry of the neighbourhood, included Lord Derby, Lord

Lathom, Captain Feilden MP, Captain Prescott and Hugh Ainscough were invited to be patrons, and the clergy vice-presidents. Mr Threlfall became president. The club opened a fortnight later with a billiards match between the president and the first member. Other activities included chess, dominoes and other games, but there do not appear to have been any women present, at least in the early days.

Throughout the 1890s the Parbold and District Agricultural Society held an annual show, originally at a site on the side of Parbold Hill, and later on a field near the station. The show had classes for horses, dogs, poultry, pigeons, flowers and produce, but not for cattle, pigs and sheep, which may reflect the nature of agriculture within the district at that time. The prizes seem remarkably generous, considering the then value of money. There were several classes for horses, for example, carrying a first prize of £2. First prize in the dog classes was 15*s*. The show was normally held in August.

The show of the older (formed about 1884) Parbold Douglas Floral and Horticultural Society was held a few weeks earlier, in July. At both of these events the Parbold Brass Band was likely to be found providing entertainment.

Although there is no cricket club in Parbold today, there was an active club in the early years of the twentieth century, playing in the Southport and District League. In the two seasons 1900 and 1901 Parbold was engaged in a number of low scoring matches, and generally emerged on the winning side, largely due to the efforts of J. Beesley and R. Lindsay, who were the mainstay of the batting, and usually were the only bowlers taking wickets. Notable performances included dismissing North Meols for nineteen; Southport St Pauls for fifteen; Southport Lancashire and Yorkshire Railways for twenty-seven and Scarisbrick Hall for ten. These victories were all in 1900. The following season Southport Lancashire and Yorkshire Railway were put out for thirty-five; Scarisbrick Hall for fifteen; Sandhurst for thirty-eight and North Meols for sixteen. The match against Newton St Marks was won by Parbold by one run. The newspaper report remarked that the large number of extras in this match was accounted for by the bumpy state of the Parbold wicket. This success was continued, and at the annual meeting of the club in 1906 it was reported that the club were champions of division one, and had won the cup for the second time in succession. When the club ceased to function has not yet been identified.

Other sporting facilities in the neighbourhood included those provided by the Douglas Lawn Tennis Club, who probably had courts in the Hilldale area, and who applied to the Rural District Council for a water supply in 1929, and the Appley Bridge Golf Club. This club, which had a nine-hole course that was actually in Parbold, with the entrance to the clubhouse from the Fairy Glen, ceased to function after the Second World War. During the 1930s they were successful enough to win the Victory Trophy, competed for by the main golf clubs of the Wigan area. Traces of the former greens and tees are still clearly visible in the meadowland below Parbold Hall. The only sporting activity still carried on in the village is that of the football club. The early history of this club has not been discovered.

During the inter-war years Parbold became well-known throughout the area as the home of the Delph Tea Gardens. This attraction, set in an old quarry, offered a café, boating lake, grottos and wooded glades, sports fields, a well-publicised fossil tree, and a motor cycle race track. It was a popular rendezvous for cyclists, Sunday School outings and general visitors who came in drives by train and coaches. Four times a year the Waterloo and District Motor Cycle Club held races on the motor cycle course, which again attracted large crowds, but was not entirely popular with local residents.

In the 1920s entertainment for young people, particularly in rural areas, was minimal and the habit grew up in Parbold for the young lads in particular to meet in Teddy Foster's newsagents in the village. He was the son of a local bargemaster, and had lost both his legs in France during the First World War. After the war he opened a shop in the village, which became so popular as a meeting place that on occasions there was little room for customers. In the end a club was formed in 1925 known as 'The Lads of the Village Club', with Mr Foster as chairman. To get funds the club held whist drives, ran a carnival and dances and was so successful that they gave hundreds of pounds to local charities. At Christmas they gave parties for the old people and the children of the village. In 1925 they formed a jazz band, and a year later a dance band. A football team was formed in 1929 to play in the Ormskirk and District League, and they won the Stanley Shield a year later. The football team, however, disbanded in 1934. In 1938 the club's activities were suspended due to lack of premises, but the Christmas party was held as usual. During 1938 and 1939 the old mill was converted into a headquarters for the club by volunteers and a billiard table was installed in March 1939. The old mill was officially opened as a clubroom on 24 May of that year. However, its further success was short-lived. With the Second World War it made way in the old mill for the Home Guard, its members became dispersed and the club was never re-formed.

The Women's Institute in Parbold was founded in about 1929. New premises were opened in November 1936 at the present site, and cost about £700. The new institute was opened by Lady Darlington, who had formerly lived in the village, and at the time had about a hundred members. It was a brave move: £400 were still owing when the official opening was held. It remains, however, as one of the few organisations to have survived the changes in social and entertainment patterns following the Second World War. Until the opening of the new community centre in the early 1970s, it was the only facility for public activities.

Postscript

PARBOLD is an unexceptional place, which until modern times had scarcely been involved in the great events of history. Yet the documents, which are the raw materials of history, are abundant and enable the researcher to build up a detailed picture of life in the township in former times. Examples of most of the different types of documents given by West in his book *Village Records* (Phillimore, 1982), can be found which directly relate to Parbold, or the mother parish of Eccleston. In this book only the surface of this mine of information has been scratched, and a wealth of detail and interpretation remains to be worked upon to develop a detailed understanding of the topics discussed in this book, as well as many others.

Selected Bibliography

A list of sources which have either been broadly and widely consulted, or which have provided useful background information. The original documentary sources consulted are listed in the References.

Victoria County History of Lancashire

John Richardson, *The Local Historian's Encyclopedia* (Historical Publications, 1981)

H. E. Tyrell, *Christ Church Douglas in Parbold*, Centenary Year, 1975

A Short History of Parbold, Parbold 1980s Onwards, Parbold Village Appraisal Committee

A Look at Parbold, Douglas Valley Historical Society, News and Reviews, No. 1, Autumn 1970.

A. Mutch, *Rural Life in South West Lancashire, 1840–1914* (Centre for North-West Regional Studies, 1988)

J. Holt, *General View of the Agriculture of the County of Lancashire* (1795)

J. M. Virgoe, *Parbold and Hilldale in Times Past* (Countryside Publications, 1988)

E. Baines, *History of Lancashire* (1870)

J. West, *Village Records* (Phillimore, 1982)

J. Lofthouse, *Lancashire's Old Families* (Hale, 1972)

W. W. Alcock, *Old Title Deeds* (Phillimore, 1986)

J. J. Bagley, *A History of Lancashire* (Phillimore, 1976)

References

Abbreviations:
LRO — Lancashire Record Office, Preston.
WRO — Wigan Record Office, Leigh.
VCH — *Victoria County History, Lancashire.*

1. A. N. Webb, *The Cartulary of Burscough Abbey*, Chetham Society (1970).
2. *The Cartulary of Cockersand Abbey*. Chetham Society (1898, 1905).
3. Jane Stirling. *Dark Age and Norman Lancashire* (Dalesman, 1973).
4. VCH, vol. vi, 178.
5. D. Mills, *The Place Names of Lancashire* (Batsford, 1976).
6. *Domesday Survey* (Phillimore).
7. J. J. Bagley, *A History of Lancashire* (Phillimore, 1976).
8. W. T. Bulpit, *Notes on Southport and District* (Southport, 1908).
9. E. Ekwall, *The Place Names of Lancashire* (MUP, 1922) (reprinted, 1972).
10. LRO DDHe 96/9.
11. LRO DDHe 126/37.
12. LRO DDHe 29/12.
13. LRO DDHe 29/4.
14. LRO DDHe 29/2.
15. J. Sephton. *A Handbook of Lancashire Place Names*. Young (Liverpool). 1913.
16. LRO DDSc 126/36.
17. LRO DDSc 126/36.
18. LRO DRB, Parbold Tithe Map, 1837.
19. W. F. Price 'Notes on Places, Traditions and Folk Lore of the Douglas Valley'. *Trans. Hist. Soc. L & C.*
20. LRO QSP 159/22.
21. LRO QSP 972/5.
22. LRO QSP 1681/23.

23. LRO QSB 1/135 (76–7).
24. LRO QSP 2121/2.
25. LRO QSP 2345/9.
26. LRO QSP 2474/2.
27. LRO QSP 2650/7.
28. LRO QSP 566.
29. LRO PR 2982 1/1.
30. R. Sharpe France. *Trans. L. & C. Antiquarian Soc.*, viii (1946).
31. 'Inquisition Thomas Lathum', *Record Soc. L. & C.*, xvii, 404–6, 1888.
32. 'Inquisition Robert Hesketh', *Record Soc. L. & C.*, xvii, 352, 1888.
33. LRO DRB, Parbold Tithe Map, 1837.
34. Lancs. Library (Skelmersdale), Census Returns 1851.
35. Lancs. Library (Skelmersdale), Census Returns 1871.
36. W. F. Price. 'Notes on Places, Traditions and Folk Lore of the Douglas Valley', *Trans. Hist. Soc. L. & C.*, xv, 181–220 (1899).
37. Peter Fleetwood-Hesketh. *Murray's Lancashire Architectural Guide* (1955).
38. LRO DP 258.
39. LRO WCW 1763.
40. WRO D/D XTa 12/14/1–2.
41. WRO D/DX Ta 43/3.
42. WRO D/DLei B2.
43. D. Anderson, *The Orrell Coalfield 1740–1850* (Moorland, 1975).
44. WRO D/DX Ta 12/16/1.
45. *Trans. Hist. Soc., L. & C.*, cx (1954), 110.
46. LRO PDR 503.
47. LRO DDX 1178/105.
48. LRO DDSc 126/36.
49. LRO MF1/27. E179/250/9.
50. 'The Registers of the Parish Church of Eccleston', *Lancs. Parish Register Soc* (1903).
51. W. T. Bulpit, *Notes on Southport and District* (Southport, 1908).
52. LRO WCW 1636.
53. LRO QSP 1661/13.
54. LRO QSP 1661/14.
55. LRO Land Tax, Leyland Hundred. QDL Parbold 1782.
56. *Record Soc. L. & C.*, xxxxvi, (1902), 120.
57. *Trans. Hist. Soc. L. & C.*, 97 (1945), 85–100.
58. *Record Soc. L. & C.*, xxx, (1895), 125–6

59. *Record Soc. L. & C.*, xxx, (1895), 114
60. WRO DDWr 539.
61. LRO DDSc 139.
62. Mark Girouard, *The Victorian Country House.*
63. LRO WCW 1759.
64. WRO DDWr 2908.
65. WRO DDWr 2335.
66. WRO DDWr 3022.
67. WRO DDWr 3043.
68. LRO QSP 513/6.
69. LRO QSP 296/20.
70. LRO QSP 325/10.
71. LRO QSP 452/28.
72. LRO QSP 291/2.
73. LRO QSP 1071/12.
74. LRO QSB 1/6 46–48.
75. LRO QSP 1222/20.
76. LRO QSP 509/9.
77. LRO QSP 517/21.
78. LRO PR 2821/8.
79. LRO DDX 285/23.
80. LRO DDX 285/1.
81. WRO DDWr 2962.
82. LRO DDX 782/2.
83. LRO DDX 782/3.
84. LRO SMPa 4.
85. WRO DDWr 2651.
86. John Sheail, *Rabbits and Their History* (David and Charles, 1971).
87. W. F. Price, *Trans. Hist. Soc. L. & C.*, xi (1895).
88. VCH, vi, 180.
89. W. F. Price, *Trans. Hist. Soc, L. & C.*, xi (1895).
90. W. F. Price, *Trans. Hist. Soc. L. & C.*, xv (1899).
91. *Discourse of the Warr in Lancashire* (Chetham Society, 1864).
92. B. G. Blackwood, *The Lancashire Gentry and the Great Rebellion 1640–60* (Chetham Society, 1978).
93. LRO QSP/27/24.
94. *Royalist Composition Papers* (Record Soc. L. & C., xxxvi, 1898), 68.
95. *Royalist Composition Papers* (Record Soc. L. & C., viii, 1883), 415.
96. B. G. Blackwood, op. cit.

97. *Lancashire Quarter Session Records* (Chetham Society, 1917).
98. W. T. Bulpit, op. cit.
99. LRO QSP 143/16.
100. LRO QSP 840/30.
101. LRO QSP 840/30.
102. LRO QSP 143/29.
103. LRO QSP 275/4.
104. LRO QSP 296/7.
105. *Record Soc. L. & C.*, (1878), 116–7.
106. LRO PR 2695/17.
107. LRO PR 175.
108. F. Walker, *Historical Geography of South West Lancashire* (Chetham Society, ciii, 1939).
109. *Record Soc. L. & C.*, xii (1885), 188–9.
110. LRO QSP 509/9.
111. LRO QSP 517/21.
112. LRO QSP 992/1.
113. The Foundation of Parbold Church in Our Lady and All Saints, Parbold, Golden Jubilee.
114. LRO DDX 1167.
115. LRO PR 2982 1/1.
116. LRO PR 3052/2/13.
117. W. F. Price 'Some Historical Notes on the Chapel of Our Blessed Lady, Parbold', *Trans. Hist. Soc., L. & C.* (1895).
118. *Southport Visiter.* Quoted in 'Parbold Church, Douglas in Parbold', Centenary Pamphlet, H. Tyrell (1975).
119. Private communication. Walker Art Gallery, 1987.
120. H. B. Rodgers, 'Land Use in Tudor Lancashire: the evidence of the final concords, 1450–1558', *Trans. Inst. Brit. Goeg.* 1955, pp. 79–97.
121. *Record Soc. L. & C.*, l.
122. *Record Soc. L. & C.*, lx.
123. WRO DDWr 3119.
124. VCH, vi, 178, note 13.
125. *Record Soc. L. & C.*, cx (1910), 56.
126. 'Inquisition of Thomas Lathom, 1623', *Record Soc. L. & C.*, (1888).
127. WRO DDWr 1405.
128. WRO DDWr 1405.
129. WRO DDWr 1410.
130. WRO DDWr 1407.

131. WRO DDWr 1396.
132. WRO MMP 25/545.
133. WRO DDWr 2586.
134. *More than a Century of Flourmilling*, H. & R. Ainscough.
135. WRO DDWr 841.
136. LRO DDSc 139.
137. LRO DDSc 141/4.
138. W. Newby, 'Tramroads in the Douglas Valley', *N. W. Soc. Ind. Arch.* ii (1977), 11.
139. J. Dandy. *History and Recollections of Tarleton* (Carnegie Press, 1985).
140. LRO DDHe 116/52.
141. LRO DDHe 116/53.
142. LRO DDHe 116/57.
143. B. Baxter *Stone Blocks and Iron Rails* (David and Charles, 1966).
144. LRO DDSc 81/1(7).
145. WRO DDWr 2572.
146. LRO DDSc 81/1(2).
147. D. Anderson, *The Orrell Coalfield Lancashire 1740–1850* (Moorland, 1975).
148. WRO D DZ A 618.
149. *Williamson's Liverpool Advertiser*, 16 Jan. 1767.
150. LRO DDSc 81/1(7).
151. Document in possession of D. Anderson. Information passed to author by J. Langton.
152. WRO DDWr 2566.
153. D. Anderson, op cit.
154. LRO DDSc 81/(7).
155. J. M. Virgoe, *British Mining Memoirs*, No. 25 (1984).
156. LRO DDHe 68/14.
157. WRO RM 1558.
158. D. Anderson. op cit.
159. Ibid.
160. WRO DDWr 3089.
161. LRO DDSc 78/3(8).
162. WRO DDWr 3117.
163. WRO DDWr 2429.
164. WRO DDWr 3004.
165. WRO, DDWr 3004.
166. Ordnance Survey 1907. Six inches to one mile.

167. LRO, DDX 1178/1–5.
168. J. M. Virgoe, *Parbold and Hilldale in Times Past* (Countryside, 1988).
169. H. E. Fitzrandolph & M. D. Hay, *The Rural Industries of England and Wales*, ii, (O.U.P., 1926) (Reprinted, 1977).
170. Ormskirk Advertiser, 1940.
171. *Ormskirk Advertiser*, 3 Dec. 1896.
172. *Ormskirk Advertiser*, 18 Feb. 1897.
173. *Wigan Observer*, 1919.
174. LRO PR 2821/1.
175. WRO RD Wi A1/1.
176. WRO RD Wi.
177. WRO RDW 2/3.
178. J. M. Virgoe, op. cit.
179. *Ormskirk Advertiser*, March 1979.
180. Peter Fleetwood-Hesketh, *Lancashire Architectural Guide* (Murray, 1955).
181. J. D. Marshall (ed.), *The History of Lancashire County Council, 1889–1974* (Martin Robertson, 1977).